Good Pope, Bad Pope

Their Lives, Our Lessons

MIKE AQUILINA

SERVANT
BOOKS

PUBLISHED BY FRANCISCAN MEDIA
Cincinnati, Ohio

Unless otherwise noted, Scripture passages have been taken from the *Revised Standard Version*, Catholic edition. Copyright 1946, 1952, 1971 by the Division of Christian Education of the National Council of Churches of Christ in the USA. Used by permission. All rights reserved.

Cover design by Candle Light Studios
Book design by Mark Sullivan

Library of Congress Cataloging-in-Publication Data
Aquilina, Mike.
Good pope, bad pope : their lives, our lessons / Mike Aquilina.
pages cm
Summary: "Why did the author pick the popes you'll meet in the pages of this book? Why not Gregory I, whom many would call the greatest pope of all time? Why not Leo X, who was pope at the beginning of the Protestant Reformation? Why not Leo XIII, who boldly stood up for the rights of workers? Every pope is by definition a remarkable man. But the popes whose stories you'll read here were chosen because they reveal how the papacy developed. They show us how Christ kept his promise to his bride, the Church, not only in her health but also in her sickness. The great popes advanced our understanding of Christian doctrine. But even more remarkable, the worst popes could do nothing to damage the teaching of the Church. That's why, even in its darkest moments, the story of the papacy is a story of triumph. And that's why it's worth knowing these twelve popes"— Provided by publisher.
ISBN 978-1-61636-628-5 (pbk.)
1. Papacy—History. 2. Popes—Biography. I. Title.
BX955.3.A68 2013
282.092'2—dc23
2013025738

ISBN 978-1-61636-628-5

Published by Servant Books, an imprint of Franciscan Media.
28 W. Liberty St.
Cincinnati, OH 45202
www.FranciscanMedia.org

Printed in the United States of America.
Printed on acid-free paper.
13 14 15 16 17 5 4 3 2 1

Contents

*W*hen in Rome I try to get to the Basilica of St. Paul Outside-the-Walls in Rome. There, one can see a long line of portraits in a frieze above the columns: Every pope who ever reigned has his face on the wall. A tourist can start at the current pope and walk back through the nineteenth century, the Renaissance, the Middle Ages, the Dark Ages, the height of the Roman Empire—and finally end at St. Peter, the rock on whom Christ built his Church.

It is a jaw-dropping experience. People have been converted to the Catholic faith just by the experience of walking past those portraits, one after the other, and seeing the unbroken line back to Peter.

Stop and think about that for a moment: We know the name of every pope, from Peter to Francis, from the first century to the twenty-first (You can find numbered lists of the names on the Internet.[1]) Does any other human institution have an unbroken succession of leaders for two thousand years?

The papacy isn't an invention of the Middle Ages or some fiction created by the Emperor Constantine. This succession of popes is historical fact—and one of the most amazing facts of history at that.

• • •

So what is the pope?

The pope is the most remarkable man on earth. And that's not because of who he is but because of what he is. The man as such may be drab and uninteresting (although very few of them really are uninteresting), but as pope he's completely unique. He is the Vicar of Christ, the visible head of the Roman Catholic Church.

The pope is also the Bishop of Rome. The two responsibilities go together. That's because St. Peter was the leader Christ chose for his Church, and he was also the first leader of the church in Rome. He passed both positions on to his successor.

While Peter was alive, everyone in the Catholic Church had to be in communion with him. Since Peter's time, being in communion with the Catholic Church has meant being in communion with the church in Rome and her bishop, the pope. That makes the pope the center— the visible source of unity for all the bishops of all the places on the face of the earth.

It's not so much that the other bishops serve under the pope as that the pope is the foundation that holds the whole structure together. The bishops are free to be Catholic leaders because they can lean on that foundation. Without Rome the other local churches would spin in all directions—as we've seen with the separated churches that reject communion with Rome.

The pope's responsibility is awe-inspiring, to say the least. The man who sits in Peter's chair—and he's just a man, like everybody else—is the head of all Christ's people on earth. Fortunately, the pope doesn't have to do it all by himself. Christ promised that the gates of hell would not prevail against his Church (see Matthew 16:18), so the pope gets the necessary help and protection when he needs it. This is what we call "papal infallibility."

What do we mean when we say the pope is infallible?

We certainly don't mean that he's always right about everything. The pope is a human being like everyone else. He may be uncommonly good. In the last few centuries, we have had more popes who were uncommonly good than otherwise. But there have been times when the pope was an uncommonly bad man. And even an uncommonly good pope can still trip over the carpet or mispronounce a word. If he falls flat on his face, he doesn't have to pick himself up, brush himself off, and say, "I meant to do that," in order to maintain the truth of papal infallibility.

Papal infallibility is something much more limited and much more comforting. Because Christ promised that the Holy Spirit would protect the Church from error—and because Christ keeps his promises—we know that when the pope, acting in his official capacity as leader of the Church, defines a doctrine that is a matter of faith or morals, he cannot teach error. But the pope can be wrong about astronomy. He can be wrong about biology. He can be wrong about all sorts of things, and—being human—he frequently is.

This distinction is important when somebody points to a notoriously corrupt pope and asks, "How can you say your pope is infallible?" No one has any trouble with the obviously good popes, the ones like St. Leo the Great, who steered the Church through perilous waters and stood up heroically for the faith against long odds. But it's really the bad popes who make the best argument for infallibility.

When we read history, it's clear that God's graces do not depend on our works. He makes his sun rise on the evil popes and on the good and sends rain on the just and on the unjust (see Matthew 5:45). Bring on the worst popes in history! If even they, with all their power, haven't been able to make a dent in Catholic truth, then it really does look as though something more than natural is going on. The Spirit really must be protecting us, because even the legendarily immoral Benedict IX and Alexander VI never managed to teach error in matters of faith and morals.

Maybe this is why Christ chose Peter, out of all the apostles, to be the first in the long line of popes. Impetuous, cowardly, bold, not always right in how he saw things, Peter was far from perfect. But with Christ's help there was nothing he couldn't do. And if Christ can make pope material out of Peter, he can do it with anyone.

• • •

Why did I choose the particular popes you'll meet in the pages of this book? Why not Gregory I, whom many would call the greatest pope of all time? Why not Leo X, who was pope at the beginning of the Protestant revolt? Why not Leo XIII, who boldly stood up for the rights of workers?

Well, believe me, I wish I could have told all their stories. Every pope is by definition a remarkable man. But I think the popes whose stories you'll read here are worth knowing because they show how the papacy developed and how Christ kept his promise to the Church not only in her health but also in her sickness. The great ones advanced our understanding of Christian doctrine, and what's even more remarkable, the worst ones could do nothing to damage the teaching of the Church.

I should admit that I have a personal reason for including John Paul II on my list. He's the only pope who ever kissed my children. I think he's interesting for other reasons too, but I wanted to be honest with you.

CHAPTER ONE

St. Peter the Apostle
(32–67)

*H*ow's this for an ugly scene?

In Antioch, just a few years after the first Christians arrived there, Peter, Christ's successor as leader of the Christian movement, is sitting at the table with some of the distinguished Christian thinkers visiting from Jerusalem. Suddenly a rather unattractive little man—a bit hunched over, balding, with a long black beard—bursts into the room. He has the look of an irate customer who has just been told that a warranty is expired. The man is Paul, that strange, interloping apostle wannabe who used to be a Pharisee of the most bigoted and persecuting type. And he has a bone to pick with Peter.

"You separate yourself from the Gentiles?" the little man demands in an unexpectedly powerful voice.

"Well…" Peter begins, but he seems a bit tongue-tied.

"You used to eat with the Gentiles," Paul continues, "until these men came up here from James in Jerusalem. Now you act like one of these guys. You've even got Barnabas doing it."

"Well, they pointed out to me that—"

Paul cuts him off. "If you, though a Jew, live like a Gentile and not like a Jew, how can you compel the Gentiles to live like Jews?" Without waiting for a reply, he turns around and stomps out.

The gentlemen from Jerusalem look at Peter, whose face is a bit red.

• • •

If you want to confront the question of infallibility head-on, you don't have to look any further than Peter. Of all the apostles, Peter seemed to be the one who failed most often. He wasn't the best educated of the apostles; that might have been Judas Iscariot, who handled the finances. He wasn't the best connected; that would be John, who had an in with the Temple authorities. He wasn't even Christ's closest personal friend; that would be John again, "the disciple whom Jesus loved" (John 19:26). Yet he was the one Christ chose to lead the Christian Church.

From the New Testament we can put together a pretty good biography of Peter. There are more stories about Peter than about all the other apostles put together. And a surprising number of them are tales of Peter's blunders.

Peter is the one who tried to walk on water and failed, the one who babbled incoherently at the Transfiguration, the one who almost refused to let Christ wash his feet, the one who swore he would never deny Christ and then did it three times, the one who used futile violence to defend Christ from the soldiers who came to arrest him, and the one who fell in with the pharisaical party, which wanted Christians to be held to the whole Law of Moses. If there was a way to botch being an apostle, Peter found it and did it.

Most of these stories are familiar to us from years of Scripture readings. But because we hear them one at a time, we seldom get a good view of the whole picture they paint. Let's start with walking on water.

[Jesus] made the disciples get into the boat and go before him to the other side, while he dismissed the crowds. And after he had dismissed the crowds, he went up on the mountain by himself to pray. When evening came, he was there alone, but the boat by this time was many furlongs distant from the land, beaten by the waves; for the wind was against them.

And in the fourth watch of the night he came to them, walking on the sea…. The disciples…were terrified, saying, "It is a ghost!"… But immediately he spoke to them, saying, "Take heart, it is I; have no fear."

And Peter answered him, "Lord, if it is you, bid me come to you on the water." He said, "Come." So Peter got out of the boat and walked on the water and came to Jesus; but when he saw the wind, he was afraid, and beginning to sink he cried out, "Lord, save me." Jesus immediately reached out his hand and caught him, saying to him, "O you of little faith, why did you doubt?"

And when they got into the boat, the wind ceased. And those in the boat worshiped him, saying, "Truly you are the Son of God." (Matthew 14:22–33)

Here's a fine example of Peter at work. He's filled with enthusiasm and thinks he can do absolutely anything. Then he starts to do it, realizes what he's attempting, and loses his nerve.

Over and over in the Gospels we see Peter go from gung ho to washout. Yet he comes up clean and dry. We see this in the foot washing at the Last Supper. Peter's first reaction is enthusiastic self-abasement: "Lord, do you wash my feet?" But as soon as Jesus tells him, "If I do not wash you, you have no part in me," Peter flops to the opposite extreme: He'll have his hands and his head washed too!

Christ's rebuke is gentle: "He who has bathed does not need to wash, except for his feet, but he is clean all over; and you are clean, but not all of you" (see John 13:5–10). We can imagine a wry smile on Jesus's face when he delivers this response, as if to say, "That's Peter for you, and we have to be patient with him."

Certainly Peter's most famous goof-up came during Jesus's hasty and illegal nocturnal trial. Jesus had warned him about it earlier, with the usual reaction from Peter: "Though they all fall away because of you, I will never fall away.… Even if I must die with you, I will not deny you" (Matthew 26:33, 35).

And then what happens?

Peter is not tortured by soldiers or threatened by burly linebacker types who could beat the tar out of him. No, all it takes to make Peter break down is somebody's maid saying he was with Jesus (see Matthew 26:69–75).

But then comes his conscience to tell him what he's done. And that's the thing that always saves Peter. When he messes up, he knows it. He doesn't rationalize or bargain or blame. He admits that he made a big mistake—even when it's a mistake from which he could think he'd never recover. "And he went out and wept bitterly" (Matthew 26:75).

• • •

None of this makes Peter sound like an ideal candidate for the position of leader for the Church. But there's another side to gung-ho Peter. His recklessness also makes him open to saying the thing no one else is ready to say, seeing the truth that no one else is ready to see. It's that very enthusiasm that brings on Christ's announcement that Peter will be the rock on which the Church is built (see Matthew 16:13–20).

Jesus asked his disciples, "Who do men say that the Son of man is?" Notice that all the other disciples were ready with answers to this first question: "Some say John the Baptist, others say Elijah, and others Jeremiah or one of the prophets." But only Peter had an answer to the next question: "Who do you say that I am?" And it was the right answer: "You are the Christ, the Son of the living God."

And Jesus answered him, "Blessed are you, Simon Bar-Jona! For flesh and blood has not revealed this to you, but my Father who is in heaven. And I tell you, you are Peter, and on this rock I will build my Church, and the gates of Hades shall not prevail against it. I will give you the keys of the kingdom of heaven, and whatever you bind on earth shall be bound in heaven, and whatever you loose on earth shall be loosed in heaven."

Peter was the conduit through which the revelation of Jesus's identity came. The Spirit was at work in him.

It will be a while before Peter learns to channel his enthusiasm properly. Just a few verses later we see him run way out of bounds.

From that time Jesus began to show his disciples that he must go to Jerusalem and suffer many things from the elders and chief priests and scribes, and be killed, and on the third day be raised. And Peter took him and began to rebuke him, saying, "God forbid, Lord! This shall never happen to you." But he turned and said to Peter, "Get behind me, Satan! You are a hindrance to me; for you are not on the side of God, but of men."

> Then Jesus told his disciples, "If any man would come after me, let him deny himself and take up his cross and follow me. For whoever would save his life will lose it, and whoever loses his life for my sake will find it." (Matthew 16:21–25)

Yet Peter's instinct was usually right. When Jesus told his followers that he was the bread of life and that they would have to eat his body and drink his blood, many of them couldn't stand the thought and walked away. "Will you also go away?" Jesus asked. Peter answered, "Lord, to whom shall we go? You have the words of eternal life; and we have believed, and have come to know, that you are the Holy One of God" (John 6:66–69).

It may be that the very thing that seems to make Peter unreliable is in fact what makes him the obvious choice to lead the Church. If the movement is going to succeed, it needs someone who will plunge forward boldly, putting all his trust in the Lord instead of his own competence.

· · ·

Peter's great love for the Lord is another quality that marks him as a great candidate for the papacy. John gives us a touching story of an interchange between Peter and Jesus after the Resurrection that shows the depth of their relationship.

> When they had finished breakfast, Jesus said to Simon Peter, "Simon, son of John, do you love me more than these?" He said to him, "Yes, Lord; you know that I love you." He said to him, "Feed my lambs." A second time he said to him, "Simon, son of John, do you love me?" He said to him, "Yes, Lord; you know that I love you." He said to him, "Tend my sheep." He said to him the third time, "Simon, son of John,

do you love me?" Peter was grieved because he said to him the third time, "Do you love me?" And he said to him, "Lord, you know everything; you know that I love you." Jesus said to him, "Feed my sheep. Truly, truly, I say to you, when you were young, you fastened your own belt and walked where you would; but when you are old, you will stretch out your hands, and another will fasten your belt for you and carry you where you do not wish to go." (This he said to show by what death he was to glorify God.) And after this he said to him, "Follow me." (John 21:15–19)

Three times Peter had denied Jesus, and it must have seemed as though there was nothing he could do to recover from that. Now Jesus is alive again and giving Peter a chance to put things right. Peter really does love Jesus—so much so that Jesus's repeating the question really exasperates him. But the exasperation, in a way, is proof of Peter's love. And he and the rest will remember what Christ tells him: If he really loves Jesus, he will take care of the people Jesus is leaving to him.

And so after Jesus ascends, Peter is in charge. We can see that he takes on the responsibility right away, without any dissent from the others. They all know what Peter is like, but not one of them questions Peter when he starts to make important decisions for the whole group.

The first important piece of business to tackle is the replacement of Judas Iscariot, and it's Peter who brings up the subject and announces the solution to the problem. He presents more than a suggestion: His is an administrative decision, not questioned by any of the other apostles. They will choose from among "the men who have accompanied us during all the time that the Lord Jesus went in and out among us" (see Acts 1:15–22).

· · ·

We don't read much in the Scriptures about Peter's personal life. We know that he was married: Christ cured his mother-in-law's fever (see Mark 1:30–31), and his wife went with him on some of his travels, as Paul mentioned to the Corinthians (see 1 Corinthians 9:5). The Acts of the Apostles concentrates on showing Peter as the leader of the Christians. And he's a very good leader—making thousands of converts with his preaching, steering the young Church through persecutions, and encouraging the others when things seem hopeless. But he's still the same old Peter who can be blown this way and that by the prevailing wind but who always recovers from his mistakes and makes things right.

In the first chapter of his Letter to the Galatians, Paul gives us a short autobiography, and much of his story is about his relationship with Peter.

Paul had been a persecutor who enthusiastically rounded up Christians and sent them off to be killed for their heresy. His vision of Christ on the road to Damascus knocked the wind out of him for some time.

When he began his career as a Christian missionary, however, Paul says, "I went up to Jerusalem to visit Cephas, and remained with him fifteen days. But I saw none of the other apostles except James the Lord's brother" (Galatians 1:18–19). Paul received his commission directly from Peter, because everyone knew that Peter was the one who had the right to give it to him.

Fourteen years later Paul was in Jerusalem again, to consult the pillars of the Church there, "James and Cephas and John" (see Galatians 2:1–10). Again, having the approval of Peter was vitally important to Paul. Without it Paul would have been "running in vain," as he says in one of his frequent sports metaphors (Galatians 2:2).

But that doesn't mean Peter was always right. And Paul was not shy about telling Peter when he was wrong. Here, in Paul's own words, is that ugly scene we imagined at the beginning of the chapter:

> But when Cephas came to Antioch I opposed him to his face, because he stood condemned. For before certain men came from James, he ate with the Gentiles; but when they came he drew back and separated himself, fearing the circumcision party. And with him the rest of the Jews acted insincerely, so that even Barnabas was carried away by their insincerity. But when I saw that they were not straightforward about the truth of the gospel, I said to Cephas before them all, "If you, though a Jew, live like a Gentile and not like a Jew, how can you compel the Gentiles to live like Jews?" (Galatians 2:11–14)

How did Peter feel about that? The words "before them all" tell us that this was a public accusation of Peter, not just a private rebuke. Doubtless every Christian in Antioch had heard the story by the next morning. "You should have seen the look on Peter's face," they must have been telling each other. "Oh, Paul's going to get it now."

But Paul was not about to back down from his position: The Gentile converts did *not* need to be circumcised, and they did *not* need to be held to the whole Law of Moses. Paul was, in fact, only reminding Peter of his own teaching: It was Peter who had received the revelation that all foods were clean (see Acts 10), and it was Peter who had declared that it was good for Christians to eat with the uncircumcised (see Acts 11:1–18). Flesh and blood had not revealed that to him.

The men from Jerusalem, on the other hand, were just as adamant on the other side: *Of course* the Gentiles had to be held to the Law of Moses. The dispute grew so heated that "Paul and Barnabas and some of the others were appointed to go up to Jerusalem to the apostles and the elders about this question" (Acts 15:2).

When they came to Jerusalem, they were welcomed by the church and the apostles and the elders, and they declared all that God had done with them. But some believers who belonged to the party of the Pharisees rose up, and said, "It is necessary to circumcise them, and to charge them to keep the law of Moses." (Acts 15:4–5)

The apostles and the elders came together, and there followed "much debate."

At this point we can picture every eye turning to Peter. It was time to make an official decision, and everyone knew that the rest of the apostles would follow Peter. And he confirmed Paul's position:

> Brethren, you know that in the early days God made choice among you, that by my mouth the Gentiles should hear the word of the gospel and believe. And God who knows the heart bore witness to them, giving them the Holy Spirit just as he did to us; and he made no distinction between us and them, but cleansed their hearts by faith. Now therefore why do you make trial of God by putting a yoke upon the neck of the disciples which neither our fathers nor we have been able to bear? But we believe that we shall be saved through the grace of the Lord Jesus, just as they will. (Acts 15:7–11)

The circumcision party was speechless. In fact, "all the assembly kept silence; and they listened to Barnabas and Paul as they related what signs and wonders God had done through them among the Gentiles" (Acts 15:12)

Once again Peter recognizes the truth and submits to it. He makes mistakes, but he always corrects them.

Maybe this is why Peter was the best choice to lead the young Church. A man who always did the right thing would set an impossibly high standard. But knowing how to recover from a mistake—that was the most valuable lesson a Christian leader could learn.

Even Christ's hand-picked leader can do the wrong thing. Certainly his successors, the popes, have done the wrong thing more than once. But the wrong wasn't allowed to continue. By the prompting of conscience or the intervention of the Holy Spirit, the Church continued on the right path.

• • •

Tradition is unanimous in saying that Peter became the leader of the Christian community in Rome. Peter himself mentions Rome by its insulting nickname "Babylon" in his first letter (1 Peter 5:13). His leadership there is why he's at the beginning of this book: Peter became the first Bishop of Rome, and because his successors inherited his position, the church of Rome stands at the head of the Catholic Church.

Peter spent much of his time teaching and preaching, telling the story of the Gospel as he remembered it. One of his star pupils was a man named Mark, who wrote down the stories he heard from Peter and gave us the Gospel According to Mark. In the varying traditions, either Peter commissioned the book, or Mark wrote it and then Peter approved it. At any rate it preserves for us the story of Jesus the way Peter told it to rapt audiences in Rome.

For most of his career as leader of the Christian Church, Peter had to confront various kinds of authorities. Jewish leaders and pagan priests would make trouble for him, and in an age when freedom of speech was not a recognized principle of government, the Roman authorities would be annoyed by the way he drew crowds of lowlifes and foreigners by his preaching. But there was no official Roman position on Christians. To outsiders the Christian movement probably seemed like yet another one of the many Jewish sects.

In the year A.D. 64 a horrendous fire destroyed as much as half the city of Rome. Rumors flew that the mad emperor Nero had deliberately set the fire, either for the fun of watching it burn or to clear some prime real estate. Indeed, Nero built his Golden House, one of the most extravagant palaces ever dreamed of, on some of the land cleared by the fire.

It was useful to have a scapegoat, so Nero blamed the fire on the Christians, who were known to believe that the fiery end of the world was near and who might be suspected of trying to hurry it up a bit. For the first time the Roman government had an official position on Christians, and that position was that Christians ought to die. Nero's thugs rounded up and killed them in various colorful ways. For example, Nero coated some of them in pitch and used them as torches to light up his garden parties.

Legend says that, as the persecution raged, Peter was persuaded to flee the city. But on the road out of Rome, he met someone going the other way. As he drew closer, he was shocked to recognize his master Jesus.

"Lord, where are you going?" Peter asked.

"I'm going to Rome to be crucified again," the Master answered. And the vision was gone.

Peter, not for the first time in his life, was ashamed of himself. He turned around and went back to Rome to face whatever God had in mind for him. And there he "stretched out his hands, and another... carried him where he did not wish to go." He was crucified upside-down, Tradition says. The inversion was Peter's own request: He didn't think he was worthy to die the same death as his Lord.

Peter's colleague Paul died on the same day, but here Paul's Roman citizenship stood him in good stead one last time. A Roman citizen couldn't be crucified, so Paul was beheaded and died instantly.

That was the end of Peter's tenure as the first pope. But it was only the beginning of the papacy, because Peter had not neglected his succession. He knew someone had to take over when he left, and he had made sure it was someone he could trust.

CHAPTER TWO

St. Clement

(first century)

*I*magine what it must have been like to follow an act like Peter's. However many times he may have goofed, Peter went out on a high note: He was a heroic martyr, an inspiration to Christians everywhere. And he was the hand-picked successor of Christ, a man who had witnessed all the great miracles of the Gospel story.

But the Church had to go on after Peter, and someone had to take over as leader. Our sources are few and a bit murky, but it seems as though Peter had ordained at least three bishops in Rome: Linus, Cletus (or Anacletus), and Clement. Some lists of popes give the order as Peter, Linus, Cletus, Clement, making Clement the fourth pope. Other sources say Clement followed right after Peter.

The confusion might be sorted out for us by the *Liber Pontificalis* (*The Book of the Popes*, an ancient Roman chronicle). Its account seems to make a distinction between the kind of bishops Linus and Cletus were and the kind of bishop Clement was.

> [Peter] ordained two bishops, Linus and Cletus, who in person fulfilled all the service of the priest in the city of Rome

for the inhabitants and for foreigners; then the blessed Peter gave himself to prayer and preaching, instructing the people.[2]

It sounds as though Linus and Cletus were what we might call auxiliary bishops, helping deal with the growing Roman congregation while Peter was still alive. A little bit later we read:

> He consecrated the blessed Clement as bishop and put the government of the see and the whole church in his hands, saying, "As my Lord Jesus Christ gave me the power to govern and bind and loose, so I hand it on to you, so that you may ordain supervisors to take care of various things who will carry on the work of the Church, and so that you may not be caught up in the cares of the world, but may give yourself solely to prayer and preaching to the people."
>
> After he had thus disposed of his affairs, he received the crown of martyrdom with Paul in the year 38 after the Lord's passion.[3]

If the *Liber Pontificalis* is right, then Clement was Peter's hand-picked successor. This sorts everything out so neatly that we hate to admit what a slender thread the *Liber Pontificalis* is to hang a theory on. It was compiled centuries later, though from earlier sources; but since it doesn't cite those sources, we have no way of knowing how reliable its traditions are. In any case, St. Clement's reign as pope—whether the second or the fourth—is well established by other historical evidence.

· · ·

We know very little about Clement as a person. One tradition suggests that he was the Titus Flavius Clemens who was a cousin of the emperor Domitian. St. Paul mentions "Clement and the rest of my fellow workers" in Philippians 4:3 as people who labored in the Church along with Euodia and Syntyche. Ancient tradition identifies this as the same Clement, and it does seem likely that Peter's hand-picked successor would have been someone who had been working in the Church for quite a while.

One thing we do know about Clement is that he was taught by the apostles themselves—particularly Peter. In his time, in fact, many of the Christians who had heard the apostles teach were still alive. It was not possible for Clement to teach anything contrary to what the apostles had taught without someone standing up to contradict him. Eusebius, the historian who tells us the story of the early Church, from the end of the New Testament to the legalization of Christianity, reminds us of that fact.

Clement, as he had seen the blessed apostles and had spent time with them, might be said to have the teaching of the apostles still sounding in his ears and what they delivered before his eyes. He was not the only one: Many others were still left who had been taught by the apostles.[4]

It's important to remember this when we hear about Clement's intervention in Corinthian affairs.

In the times of this Clement, there was a great dispute among the brethren at Corinth. On that occasion the church at Rome wrote a considerable letter to the Corinthians, confirming them in peace and renewing their faith and the teaching they had lately received from the apostles.[5]

The thing for which Clement is most remembered is this letter to Corinth. It's one of the earliest extant Christian writings outside the New Testament. Eusebius wrote:

> One letter of this Clement still exists that is acknowledged
> as genuine. It is fairly long and of great merit. He wrote it in

the name of the church at Rome to the church in Corinth, when there was a dispute in the latter church. We know that this letter has been publicly read for common benefit in most of the churches, both in former times and in our own. Hegesippus clearly bears witness that there was in fact a sedition at Corinth at the time of the letter.[6]

Even a century after it was written, the letter was standard reading in the Corinthian church. Eusebius mentions a letter of Dionysius, a later bishop of Corinth, in which he thanks Pope Soter (pope from 166 to 174) for a letter he had sent to Corinth: "Today we have passed the Lord's holy day, in which we have read your letter. In reading it we shall always have our minds stored with admonition, as we do from the one written to us before by Clement."[7] That tells us how much the Corinthians thought of Clement's letter.

What's important for us here is what this letter says about Clement's position in the Church. He begins (writing in the name of the church in Rome) the way countless writers over the centuries have begun their letters: by apologizing for not having written sooner.

Because of the sudden calamities that have happened to me one after another, we feel as though we've taken too long to turn my attention to the points on which you consulted me—and especially to that shameful and detestable sedition, utterly abhorrent to the elect of God, which a few rash and self-confident persons have kindled to such a pitch of frenzy, that your venerable and illustrious name, worthy to be loved everywhere, has been seriously injured.[8]

From this short paragraph we get a very clear idea of what's going on. The Corinthians are fighting again. We remember how Paul had to take them to task for their bickering: "For it has been reported to me by Chloe's people that there is quarreling among you, my brethren" (1 Corinthians 1:11). Apparently it was a quarrelsome congregation. Someone in Corinth had written to Clement and asked him to sort out the current argument.

Now, why would the Corinthians write to the Bishop of Rome with questions about a purely local matter? There can be only one reason: As the successor to Peter, Clement had responsibility not only for the local church in Rome but for the whole Christian Church.

This is a very important point. No one in mainstream scholarship seriously doubts the authenticity of this letter. The date is pretty well established as before the year A.D. 100. And it is very clear from the letter that the church in Corinth had turned to Rome to deal with what the local church had failed to sort out. This is evidence that the Bishop of Rome was exercising authority over the other local churches in the generation immediately after Peter. Peter's authority over the whole Christian Church passed to his successor in Rome, and the Corinthian church recognized that fact.

• • •

As we might expect, Clement's letter puts great stress on the unity of the Church. We're all in this together, says Clement, and it's important not to let petty ambitions get in the way.

> We write these things to you, dear friends, not only to admonish you of your duty but also to remind ourselves. For we are struggling in the same arena, and the same conflict is assigned to both of us….
>
> It is right and holy therefore, men and brethren, to obey God rather than follow those who, through pride and sedition,

have become the leaders of a detestable ambition. For we shall incur no slight injury, but rather great danger, if we rashly yield ourselves to the inclinations of men who aim at exciting strife and tumults, so as to draw us away from what is good. Let us be kind one to another after the pattern of the tender mercy and goodness of our Creator.[9]

The key to this unity is humility. Instead of trying to puff themselves up into something greater than they are, Christians should simply be happy to do what is right.

Let our whole body, then, be preserved in Christ Jesus; and let everyone be subject to his neighbor, according to the special gift bestowed upon him. Let the strong not despise the weak, and let the weak show respect to the strong. Let the rich man provide for the wants of the poor; and let the poor man bless God, because God has given him someone by whom his need may be supplied. Let the wise man display his wisdom, not by words but through good deeds. Let the humble not blow his own trumpet but leave witness to be borne to him by another. Let anyone who is pure in the flesh not grow proud of it and boast, knowing that it was another who gave him the gift of continence.[10]

What right does Clement have to tell the Corinthians these things? Well, they asked him.

Clement puts a lot of effort into showing that there is a proper order in the Church. The apostles got their knowledge from Christ, and the bishops from the apostles. Christ appointed the apostles, and the apostles appointed the bishops.

The apostles have preached the Gospel to us from the Lord Jesus Christ, and Jesus Christ from God. Christ therefore was sent forth by God, and the apostles by Christ. Both these appointments, then, were made in an orderly way, according to the will of God. So when the apostles had received their orders, and had been fully assured by the resurrection of our Lord Jesus Christ and established in the word of God with full assurance of the Holy Spirit, they went forth proclaiming that the kingdom of God was at hand.

And thus preaching through countries and cities, they appointed their first fruits, having first proved them by the Spirit, to be bishops and deacons of those who would believe in later times. Nor was this any new thing, since indeed many ages before it was written concerning bishops and deacons. For this is what Scripture says somewhere: "I will appoint their bishops in righteousness, and their deacons in faith" [compare Isaiah 60:17]....[11]

The order doesn't end with the generation after the apostles. It's important that it should continue generation after generation

Our apostles also knew, through our Lord Jesus Christ, that there would be strife on account of the office of bishop. For this reason, therefore, since they had been given a perfect foreknowledge of this, they appointed the successors I already mentioned and afterwards gave instructions that when those men should fall asleep, other approved men should succeed them in their ministry.[12]

Since the present bishops are part of a succession that goes right back through the apostles to Christ, Clement continues, they can't be tossed aside on a whim. This is the serious mistake the Corinthians are making.

I am of the opinion, therefore, that those appointed by [the apostles], or afterwards by other eminent men, with the consent of the whole church, and who have blamelessly served the flock of Christ, in a humble, peaceable, and disinterested spirit, and have for a long time possessed the good opinion of all, cannot be justly dismissed from the ministry. For our sin will not be small if we eject from the episcopate those who have fulfilled its duties in a blameless and holy way. Blessed are those priests who, having finished their course before now, have earned a fruitful and perfect departure; for they have no fear that anyone might deprive them of the place now appointed them. But I see that you have removed some men of excellent behavior from the ministry, which they fulfilled blamelessly and with honor....

But now reflect who those are that have perverted you and lessened the renown of your famous brotherly love. It is disgraceful, beloved, yea, highly disgraceful, and unworthy of your Christian profession, that such a thing should be heard of as that the most steadfast and ancient church of the Corinthians should, on account of one or two persons, engage in sedition against its priests. And this rumor has reached not only me but also those who are unconnected with me; so that, through your infatuation, the name of the Lord is blasphemed, while danger is also brought upon yourselves.

Let us therefore, with all haste, put an end to this; and let us fall down before the Lord, and beseech Him with tears, that

He would mercifully be reconciled to us and restore us to our former seemly and holy practice of brotherly love.[13]

The solution to the problem, Clement reiterates, is humility.

> You who laid the foundation of this sedition, submit yourselves to the priests, and let them give you correction so that you repent, bending the knees of your hearts. Learn to be subject, laying aside the proud and arrogant self-confidence of your tongue. For it is better for you that you should occupy a humble but honorable place in the flock of Christ than that, being highly exalted, you should be cast out from the hope of his people.[14]

Clement expected nothing short of the "obedience" that was due his office because of its divine assistance and guarantees. "You will give us great joy and gladness," he wrote, "if you render obedience to the things *written by us through the Holy Spirit.*"

· · ·

How did Clement's letter go over in Corinth? We don't know exactly what happened when it got there—whether, for example, the malcontents repented and submitted themselves to the priests the way Clement told them to do. We'd like to think they did.

What we do know is that the letter was still being read in the church of Corinth a century after Clement wrote it. Certainly the Corinthians didn't think Clement had overstepped his authority; on the contrary, they counted the letter from Peter's successor among their greatest treasures.

The rest of Clement's life is shrouded in legend and obscurity. Long tradition says that he was finally exiled to the Crimea, where he annoyed the local officials by converting a large number of the pagan population. To get rid of the troublemaker, the officials tied an anchor around his neck and tossed him into the Black Sea. This tradition is nearly universal in the Church, but we don't have any early evidence for it; no one mentions it before the 300s.

The details of his life are not what matter about Pope Clement. What does matter is that he brought Peter's authority forward into the next generation—and passed it on to his successors. In Clement we see the successor of Peter in Rome acting as pope.

CHAPTER THREE

Liberius
(352–356)

*W*hen Constantine became emperor in AD 312, everything in the Roman Empire was upended. Constantine had converted to Christianity shortly before his reign began, so Christianity suddenly went from an illegal cult to the favored religion of the empire. Religious freedom, for the first time anywhere, was the law. (That didn't last; the next generation of emperors began a long process of clamping down on and finally extinguishing paganism.)

But what was Christianity? Heresies—false teachings and splinter sects—had popped up everywhere. The most popular of them all was Arianism, named for its founder, Arius, who taught that the Son had been created in time and was not equal to the Father.

To sort everything out, Constantine called all the bishops together at Nicaea in 325. They condemned the teachings of Arius and came up with a statement of the orthodox faith—the first version of what we call the Nicene Creed. The Arians, though temporarily discouraged, rallied and found a foothold in the imperial palace. By the time Liberius became pope in 352, during the reign of Constantine's son

Constantius, the Arians had the imperial ear, and orthodox bishops were losing their sees.

. . .

The one Christian who stood up for orthodoxy more consistently and stubbornly than any other was St. Athanasius, bishop of Alexandria. As a young man of twenty-seven, he had been one of the leaders of the orthodox side at the Council of Nicaea. After that he was a constant thorn in the side of the Arians. Constantius arranged for a captive synod to excommunicate Athanasius on trumped-up charges, but Liberius refused to separate himself from the champion of orthodoxy.

We have a fairly complete record of everything that went on, written by someone who certainly qualifies as an insider. Athanasius's history of the Arian heresy tells us the whole story of poor old Liberius. Naturally, Athanasius had his prejudices, and we have to assume that many of the conversations he recorded were just his best guesses as to what the people he knew might have said. But he does give us the whole story of Liberius's combat with the Arians—a combat the pope nearly lost.

The first thing that was shocking about the way Liberius was treated, as far as Athanasius was concerned, was the simple fact that he was Bishop of Rome. You don't treat the pope with disrespect—even if you're the emperor of the world.

Now it would have been better if from the first Constantius had never become connected with this heresy at all; or if he had been connected with it, if he had not yielded so much to those impious men; or if he had yielded to them, if he had stood by them only so far, so that judgment might come upon them all for these atrocities alone. But it seems that, like madmen, having fixed themselves in the bonds of impiety, they are drawing down upon their own heads a more severe judgment.

Thus from the first they spared not even Liberius, Bishop of Rome, but extended their fury even to those parts. They did not respect his bishopric because it was an Apostolic throne. They felt no reverence for Rome because she is the Metropolis of the Roman Empire. They did not remember that in their letters they used to speak of her Bishops as apostolic men. But confusing everything together, they forgot everything at once, and cared only to show their zeal in behalf of impiety.

When they saw that [Athanasius] was an orthodox man and hated the Arian heresy, and earnestly tried to persuade everyone to renounce and withdraw from it, these impious men reasoned thus with themselves: "If we can persuade Liberius, we shall soon prevail over all." So they accused him falsely before the emperor. The emperor expected that he would easily bring everyone over to his side by means of Liberius, so he wrote to him and sent a certain eunuch called Eusebius with letters and offerings—to cajole him with the presents and to threaten him with the letters.[15]

This Eusebius (not the one I cited earlier) was one of the great villains of history. He had risen to a high position under Constantine and from there schemed and killed his way into more and more influence in the imperial court. He made a profitable business of accusing rich men of treason and then confiscating their estates when they were executed. And it was Eusebius who, more than anyone else, had propagated the Arian heresy in the imperial court. When we hear Athanasius speaking of the Arians as if they were capable of any wickedness, we have to remember that the prime mover in all the Arian schemes against Athanasius was Eusebius, who really was capable of any wickedness.

Constantius seems to have thought that everything would be perfectly all right if he could just get rid of that firebrand Athanasius. Even though he did not doubt his authority to deal with Athanasius, he recognized that there were many orthodox Christians who would not see things his way. If the pope could be brought to condemn Athanasius, the emperor reasoned, then the victory was practically won. Obviously even a heretical emperor saw how things stood in the Christian Church: You don't carry the day unless the pope is on your side.

The eunuch therefore went to Rome, and first proposed to Liberius to subscribe against Athanasius, and to hold communion with the Arians, saying, "The Emperor wishes it, and commands you to do so." And then showing him the offerings, he took him by the hand, and again besought him saying, "Obey the Emperor, and you'll get these."[16]

Pope Liberius, however, was not to be won over by threats and bribes.

The Bishop tried to convince [Eusebius], reasoning with him this way: "How is it possible for me to do this against Athanasius? How can we condemn a man whom not one Council only but a second, assembled from all parts of the world, has fairly acquitted, and whom the Church of the Romans dismissed in peace? Who will approve of our conduct if we reject in his absence one whose presence among us we gladly welcomed, and admitted him to our communion? This is no Ecclesiastical Canon; nor have we had transmitted to us any such tradition from the Fathers, who in their turn received from the great and blessed Apostle Peter."[17]

Liberius presented a simple counterproposal for the emperor: Summon another council, holding it far from imperial interference. Let the Church be influenced by nothing but the Holy Spirit, and we'll see whether Athanasius is right or wrong.

These were not the words Eusebius wanted to hear.

And the eunuch, who was vexed, not so much because Liberius would not subscribe as because he found Liberius an enemy to the heresy, forgot that he was in the presence of a Bishop. After threatening him severely, the eunuch went away with the offerings; he next committed an offense that is foreign to a Christian and too audacious for a eunuch. In imitation of the transgression of Saul, he went to the Martyry of the Apostle Peter and presented the offerings.

When Liberius heard about it, he was very angry with the person who kept the place, because he had not prevented Eusebius, and [Liberius] cast out the offerings as an unlawful sacrifice—which increased the anger of the mutilated creature against him.

Consequently [Eusebius] exasperated the Emperor against [Liberius], saying, "The matter that concerns us is no longer obtaining the subscription of Liberius but the fact that he is so resolutely opposed to the heresy that he anathematizes the Arians by name." He also stirred up the other eunuchs to say the same; for many of those who were around Constantius, or rather the whole number of them, were eunuchs, who absorbed all the influence with him, and it was impossible to do anything there without them. The Emperor accordingly wrote to Rome, and again Palatines and Notaries and Counts were sent off with letters to the Prefect, in order that they might either inveigle Liberius by stratagem away from Rome and send him to the Court ... or else persecute him by violence.[18]

. . .

Then began a reign of terror in Rome. Arian schemers, with the emperor on their side, made life impossible for the orthodox community—all for the sake of making Liberius miserable! Such being the tenor of the letters, fear and treachery immediately became rife throughout the whole city. How many families were threatened! How many received great promises on condition of their acting against Liberius! How many bishops hid themselves when they saw these things! How many noble women retired to country places because of the slanders of the enemies of Christ! How many ascetics were made the objects of their plots! How many who were sojourning there, and had made that place their home, did they cause to be persecuted! How often and how strictly did they guard the harbor and the approaches to the gates, lest any orthodox person should enter and visit Liberius! Rome at last had experience of the enemies of Christ and now understood what before she would not believe when she heard how the other churches in every city were ravaged by them.[19]

None of this oppression worked. Liberius would not condemn Athanasius. When called before Constantius in the imperial capital of Milan, Liberius accused the emperor of being a persecutor like the old pagan emperors.

"Stop persecuting the Christians," [Liberius] said. "Do not try to introduce impiety into the Church in any way. We are ready to suffer anything rather than to be called Arian madmen. We are Christians; do not make us become enemies of Christ. We also give you this advice: do not fight against the One who gave you this empire, or show impiety toward him instead of thankfulness. Do not persecute those who believe in him, or you might also hear the words, 'It is hard for you to kick against the pricks' [Acts 9:5; this last part of the verse does not appear in all manuscripts]. In fact, I wish you would hear them, so that you might obey, as the holy Paul did. Behold, here we are; we have come, before they make up false charges. For this cause we hastened hither, knowing that banishment awaits us at your hands, so that we might suffer before a charge encounters us, and so that all may clearly see that all the others too have suffered as we shall suffer, and that the charges brought against them were fabrications of their enemies, and all their proceedings were mere calumny and falsehood."[20]

Constantius had had enough of this stubbornness. He was ready to show everyone that they must not defy a Roman emperor to his face. He imposed a sentence of banishment on those who opposed him—and not just banishment but solitary banishment.

The Emperor…had…devised this plan of separation…so that the severity of his punishments might be greater than that of former tyrants and persecutors.…[H]e put asunder those who were united by the bond of faith, that when they came to die they might not see one another—thinking that bodily separation can disunite also the affections of the mind, and that being separated from each other, they would forget the agreement and unanimity that existed among them. He did not know that, however each one may remain apart from the rest, he has nevertheless with him that Lord, whom they confessed in one body together, who will also provide—as he did in the case of the Prophet Elisha [2 Kings 6:16]—that more shall be with each of them than there are soldiers with Constantius. Certainly iniquity is blind![21]

. . .

We have a record of this interview between Constantius and Liberius from another source, the historian Theodoret. The dialogue may have been copied from official transcripts. (The Roman Empire had a huge and bloated bureaucracy; there would have been official transcripts of everything.) We can see that Liberius held out bravely, though perhaps not quite as defiantly as Athanasius imagined. He tried to reason with the emperor more than defy him.

Constantius: We have judged it right, as you are a Christian and the bishop of our city, to send for you in order to admonish you to abjure all connection with the folly of the impious Athanasius. For when he was separated from the communion of the Church by the synod, the whole world approved of the decision.

Liberius: O Emperor, ecclesiastical sentences ought to be enacted with strictest justice: therefore, if it please your piety, order the court to be assembled, and if turns out that Athanasius deserves condemnation, then let sentence be passed upon him according to ecclesiastical forms. For it is not possible for us to condemn a man unheard and untried.

Constantius: The whole world has condemned his impiety; but he, as he has done from the first, laughs at the danger.

Liberius: Those who signed the condemnation were not eyewitnesses of anything that occurred, but were moved by the desire of glory and by the fear of disgrace at your hands.

Constantius: What do you mean by glory and fear and disgrace?

Liberius: Those who do not love the glory of God, but who attach greater value to your gifts, have condemned a man whom they have neither seen nor judged; this is very contrary to the principles of Christians.

Constantius: Athanasius was tried in person at the council of Tyre, and all the bishops of the world at that synod condemned him.

Liberius: No judgment has ever been passed on him in his presence. Those who there assembled condemned him after he had left.

Eusebius the Eunuch: It was demonstrated at the council of Nicaea that he held opinions entirely at variance with the Catholic faith.

Liberius: Of all those…sent for the purpose of drawing up memorials against the accused, only five delivered the sentence against him….. Sentence was passed at Sardica against all those who were sent for this purpose to Mareotis. They presented a petition to the council soliciting pardon for having drawn up at Mareotis memorials against Athanasius, consisting of false accusations and depositions of only one party. Their petition is still in our hands. Whose cause are we to take up, Emperor? With whom are we to agree and hold communion? With those who first condemned Athanasius, and then solicited pardon for having condemned him, or with those who have condemned the ones who asked for pardon?

Epictetus the [Arian] Bishop: O Emperor, Liberius is not pleading on behalf of the faith or in defense of ecclesiastical judgments, but only because he wants to boast before the Roman senators that he beat the emperor in an argument.

Constantius (to Liberius): How much of the universe do you take up, that you alone by yourself stand by an impious man, and are destroying the peace of the empire and of the whole world?

Liberius: The fact that I stand alone does not make the truth the least bit weaker. According to the ancient story, there are found only three men resisting a decree [see Daniel 3:12].

Eusebius the Eunuch: You make our emperor a Nebuchadnezzar!

Liberius: Certainly not. But you rashly condemn a man without any trial. What I desire is, in the first place, that a general confession of faith be signed, confirming that drawn up at the council of Nicaea. And secondly, that all our brothers be recalled from exile, and reinstated in their own bishoprics. If, when all this has been carried into execution, it can be shown that the doctrines of all those who now fill the churches with trouble are conformable to the apostolic faith, then we will all assemble at Alexandria to meet the accused, the accusers, and their defender, and after having examined the cause, we will pass judgment upon it.

Epictetus the Bishop: There will not be enough post-carriages to carry so many bishops! [These "post-carriages" were government transports, to be used on official business only.]

Liberius: Ecclesiastical affairs can be transacted without post-carriages. The churches have enough money for the transportation of their own bishops to the sea coast.

Constantius: The sentence that has once been passed ought not to be revoked. The decision of the greater number of bishops ought to prevail. You alone retain friendship towards that impious man.

Liberius: Emperor, it is a thing unheard of till now that a judge should accuse the absent of impiety, as if he were his personal enemy.

Constantius: All without exception have been injured by him, but none so deeply as I have been. Not content with the death of my eldest brother, he never ceased to excite Constans, of blessed memory, to enmity against me. But I, with much moderation, put up alike with the vehemence of both the instigator and his victim. Not one of the victories I have gained, not even excepting those over Magnentius and Silvanus,... equals expelling this vile man from the government of the Church.

The "eldest brother" was Constantine II, who died after he was surrounded by the troops of a younger brother, Constans "of blessed memory," in a brief civil war between the two. Magnentius and Silvanus were two usurpers who tried to take over the imperial throne but were defeated by Constantius; Magnentius had killed Constans, and his defeat left Constantius as sole ruler of the empire. It is a remarkable testimony to the importance of Christian theology in the empire that the emperor would be prouder of firing the bishop of Alexandria than he would be of conquering the usurper who killed his brother.

Liberius: Do not use bishops to vindicate your own hatred and revenge, Emperor, for their hands ought only to be raised for purposes of blessing and of sanctification. If it is consonant with your will, command the bishops to return to their own residences; and if it appears that they are of one mind with him who today maintains the true doctrines of the confession of faith signed at Nicaea, then let them come together and see to the peace of the world, in order that an innocent man may not serve as a mark for reproach.

Constantius: There is only one question left to ask. I wish you to enter into communion with the churches and to send you back to Rome. Consent therefore to peace, and sign your assent, and then you can go back to Rome.

Liberius: I have already said good-bye to the brethren in that city. The decrees of the Church are of greater importance than living in Rome.

Constantius: You have three days to consider whether you will sign the document and return to Rome; if not, you must choose the place of your banishment.

Liberius: Neither three days nor three months can change my sentiments. Send me wherever you please.[22]

Liberius continued defiant. After the three days the emperor banished him to Beroea, a city of Thrace. Liberius couldn't resist an opportunity to put the emperor in his place.

Upon the departure of Liberius, the emperor sent him five hundred pieces of gold to defray his expenses. Liberius said to the messenger who brought them, "Go and give them back to the emperor. He needs them to pay his troops."

The empress also sent him a sum of the same amount; he said, "Take it to the emperor, for he may want it to pay his troops; but if not, let it be given to Auxentius and Epictetus [two of the Arian bishops who had condemned Liberius], for they certainly need it."

Eusebius the eunuch brought him other sums of money, and he thus addressed him: "You have turned all the churches of the world into a desert, and now you bring alms to me, as if I were a criminal? Go away, and first become a Christian."[23]

• • •

An interesting version of this story comes from Ammianus Marcellinus, a pagan historian who was a government insider at the time. He could never conceal his contempt for the Christians, and he swallowed all the false accusations against Athanasius, but even he finds Liberius acting nobly when faced with the unreasonable demands of Constantius. Furthermore, he acknowledges that the emperor, "being always unfavorable to Athanasius, although he knew that what he ordered had already been done, yet very much wanted to have it confirmed by that authority that the bishops of the Eternal City enjoy, as being of higher rank."[24]

When a pagan who hates Christians speaks of papal authority in this way, we know that he isn't speaking from some sectarian prejudice. He's just calling 'em like he sees 'em.

Athanasius picks up our story again, telling us how cruelly the friends of Liberius were persecuted.

Who can hear what they did in the course of these proceedings without thinking them to be *anything* rather than Christians? When Liberius sent Eutropius, a priest, and Hilarius, a deacon, with letters to the Emperor, at the time that Lucifer and his fellows made their confession, they banished the priest on the spot, and after stripping Hilarius the deacon and scourging him on the back, they banished him too, shouting at him, "Why didn't you resist Liberius instead of bringing letters from him?"

....The deacon, while he was being scourged, praised the Lord, remembering his words, "I gave My back to the smiters" [Isaiah 50:6]. But they laughed and mocked him while they scourged him, feeling no shame that they were insulting a Levite. Indeed they merely acted consistently in laughing while he continued to praise God; for it is the part of Christians to endure stripes, but to scourge Christians is the outrage of a Pilate or a Caiaphas. Thus they endeavored at the first to corrupt the Church of the Romans, wishing to introduce impiety into it as well as others.[25]

Beroea was not a pleasant place, and in spite of his brave resistance, banishment took its toll on Liberius. The emperor's minions kept up the pressure on him and more than once hinted that banishment was too good for the appalling crime of defying the emperor's command. If it didn't bring him to his senses, there were other things they could try.

Liberius had been two years away from Rome when he cracked. Athanasius doesn't blame Liberius at all for giving up, even though it led to Athanasius's excommunication. He understands what torture Liberius went through—Athanasius had had more than his fair share of banishments himself and was in exile yet again when he wrote his history—and only blames the people who tortured him. True to his principles, he treats the Bishop of Rome with the greatest respect.

But after he had been in banishment two years, Liberius gave way, and from fear of threatened death subscribed. Yet even this only shows their violent conduct, and the hatred of Liberius against the heresy, and his support of Athanasius, so long as he was suffered to exercise a free choice. For that which men are forced by torture to do contrary to their first judgment ought not to be considered the willing deed of those who are in fear, but rather of their tormentors. They however attempted everything in support of their heresy, while the people in every Church, preserving the faith that they had learned, waited for the return of their teachers, and condemned the Antichristian heresy, and all avoid it, as they would a serpent.

Who that saw when Liberius, Bishop of Rome, was banished, and when the great Hosius, the father of the Bishops, suffered these things, or who that saw so many Bishops banished out of Spain and the other parts, could fail to perceive, however little sense he might possess, that the charges against Athanasius and the rest were also false, and nothing but mere calumny? For this reason those others also endured all suffering, because they saw plainly that the conspiracies laid against these were founded in falsehood. For what charge was there against Liberius? Or what accusation against the aged Hosius? Who bore even a false witness against Paulinus, and Lucifer, and

Dionysius, and Eusebius? Or what sin could be lain to the account of the rest of the banished Bishops, and Presbyters, and Deacons? None at all; God forbid. There were no charges against them on which a plot for their ruin might be formed; nor was it on the ground of any accusation that they were separately banished. It was an insurrection of impiety against godliness; it was zeal for the Arian heresy and a prelude to the coming of Antichrist, for whom Constantius is thus preparing the way.[26]

. . .

We don't exactly know what Liberius agreed to in order to end his exile. Excommunication of Athanasius was part of it. And it seems he was forced to sign some sort of compromise statement that did not literally deviate from orthodox doctrine but could also be interpreted as satisfying the Arians.

Liberius returned to Rome in triumph. (The Roman mob probably didn't know he had condemned Athanasius.) In his absence another pope—now remembered as the antipope Felix—had been appointed, and with his usual instinct for compromise, Constantius wanted the two bishops to rule jointly. But the Romans would have none of that. "One God, one Christ, one bishop!" they shouted in the streets. Felix was run out of town.

When we look back at Liberius and his excommunication of Athanasius, we have to keep in mind that the charism of infallibility applies to doctrine, not disciplinary actions. As Catholic Christians we believe that the pope is protected by the Holy Spirit when he defines doctrine by virtue of his office as pope. But when he disciplines a bishop or makes an administrative decision, he's using his best human judgment or, in the case of Liberius, caving in to extreme deprivation and duress.

Even at his lowest point, Liberius carefully avoided proclaiming Arian doctrine. Though weakened by duress, he was not heretical. Interestingly enough, even Felix the antipope, though he consented to recall the Arian bishops, taught only orthodox Catholic doctrine.

The Holy Spirit kept Christ's promise. At the end of Liberius's difficult life, the orthodox Catholic faith was still intact. The best efforts of the Roman emperor, the most powerful man in the world, could not change the teaching of the Catholic Church.

History remembers Athanasius as a saint. No one has ever venerated Liberius. But he was a pope, and that counts for something. In spite of all his troubles, he passed the faith on safely to his successors.

CHAPTER FOUR

Damasus
(366–384)

W hen Liberius died, the papacy was not just a position of responsibility in the Church. Now that Christianity was the favored religion of the empire, the chair of Peter was one of the greatest prizes an ambitious Roman could hope to win. Damasus was the next to occupy it, though there was some contention.

> A deacon named Ursinus, having obtained some votes in his favor, caused himself to be clandestinely ordained by some bishops of little note and tried to create a division among the people, so as to form separate assemblies. He succeeded in creating this division, and some of the people followed him, while the rest stayed with Damasus. This gave rise to many disputes, and to much contention, which at length proceeded to murder and bloodshed. The prefect of Rome was obliged to interfere, and to punish many of the clergy and people; and he put an end to the usurpation of Ursinus. With respect to doctrine, however, no dissension arose either at Rome or in

any other of the Western churches. The people unanimously adhered to the form of belief established at Nicaea, and regarded the three Persons of the Trinity as equal in dignity and in power.[27]

Those last two sentences are especially interesting in the history of the papacy. They show us that the city of Rome was a haven of orthodoxy. Although two men were fighting over the see of Rome, and although mobs were warring in the streets, there were no differences in doctrine. This steadiness helped Rome keep its providential place at the head of the Church.

Our pagan friend Ammianus Marcellinus finds the fight between the rival mobs revolting, as well he might. He can't distinguish the sides; all he knows is that there are riots in the streets and people killed. He may have heard exaggerated numbers, but there's no question that people are killing each other over the choice of a new bishop. That didn't make Ammianus think any better of the Christians.

Damasus and Ursinus, being both immoderately eager to obtain the bishopric, formed parties and carried on the conflict with great bitterness, the partisans of each carrying their violence to actual battle, in which men were wounded and killed. And as Juventius [prefect of the city] was unable to put an end to these disorders, or even to soften them, he was at last by their violence compelled to withdraw to the suburbs.

Ultimately Damasus got the best of the strife by the strenuous efforts of his partisans. It is certain that on one day one hundred and thirty-seven dead bodies were found in the Basilica of Sicininus, which is a Christian church. And the populace who had been thus roused to a state of ferocity were with great difficulty restored to order.[28]

Ammianus is not surprised that ambitious men should covet the papacy. His outsider's picture of the popes proves beyond doubt how much their influence had grown in the world.

> I do not deny, when I consider the ostentation that reigns at Rome, that those who desire such rank and power may be justified in laboring with all possible exertion and vehemence to obtain their wishes—since after they have succeeded, they will be set for life, being enriched by offerings from matrons, riding in carriages, dressing splendidly, and feasting luxuriously, so that their entertainments surpass even royal banquets.

> And they might be really happy if, despising the vastness of the city, which they excite against themselves by their vices, they were to live in imitation of some of the priests in the provinces, whom the most rigid abstinence in eating and drinking, and plainness of apparel, and eyes always cast on the ground, recommend to the everlasting Deity and his true worshipers as pure and sober-minded men.[29]

• • •

But who was this Damasus? He was apparently a cultured man, as his friend St. Jerome tells us: "Damasus, bishop of Rome, had a fine talent for making verses and published many brief works in heroic meter."[30] He might have contributed to classical literature if he had had more time, but he had few moments to spare.

The defining conflict of Damasus's time was the Arian heresy, which had spread throughout the Eastern half of the empire and was beginning to infect the West as well. As we saw with Liberius, the faithful everywhere looked to the Bishop of Rome for authoritative decisions.

Things started to look up when Gratian became emperor. As the historian Theodoret tells us, Gratian was altogether orthodox, and he brought back all the bishops who had been exiled by previous Arian administrations. It's worth noting that, as far as the emperor's edict was concerned, the test of a bishop's orthodoxy was whether he was in communion with Damasus, the Bishop of Rome.

> The emperor at once gave plain indications of his adherence to true religion, and offered the first fruits of his kingdom to the Lord of all, by publishing an edict commanding the exiled shepherds to return and to be restored to their flocks, and ordering the sacred buildings to be delivered to congregations adopting communion with Damasus.

> This Damasus, the successor of Liberius in the see of Rome, was a man of most praiseworthy life and by his own choice alike in word and deed a champion of Apostolic doctrines. To put his edict in force Gratian sent Sapor the general, a very famous character at that time, with orders to expel the preachers of the blasphemies of Arius, like wild beasts from the sacred folds, and to effect the restoration of the excellent shepherds to God's flocks.[31]

This was all very good for the orthodox side. But in Antioch—one of the chief cities of the empire—there were difficult problems to sort out. When the bishops of Antioch had been Arian, the orthodox faithful had refused to recognize them. But the orthodox, lacking official support, had not been able to agree on a bishop. Now there were three men claiming to be the Catholic bishop of Antioch. Once again, all three knew what the test of true Catholic status was, so they all claimed to be in communion with Damasus.

Paulinus affirmed that he sided with Damasus, and Apollinarius, concealing his unsoundness, did the same. The divine Meletius, on the other hand, made no sign, and put up with their dispute. Flavianus, of high fame for his wisdom, who was at that time still in the ranks of the presbyterate, at first said to Paulinus in the hearing of the officer, "If, my dear friend, you accept communion with Damasus, point out to us clearly how the doctrines agree, for he though he owns one substance of the Trinity openly preaches three essences. You on the contrary deny the Trinity of the essences. Show us then how these doctrines are in harmony, and receive the charge of the churches, as the edict enjoins."

After so silencing Paulinus by his arguments, he turned to Apollinarius and said, "I am astonished, my friend, to find you waging such violent war against the truth, when all the while you know quite clearly how the admirable Damasus maintains our nature to have been taken in its perfection by God the Word; but you persist in saying the contrary, for you deprive our intelligence of its salvation. If these our charges against you be false, deny now the novelty that you have originated; embrace the teaching of Damasus, and receive the charge of the holy shrines."[32]

• • •

In spite of the wise words of Flavius, the dispute dragged on. The difficulties in Antioch were especially disturbing to one of the greatest theologians of the age, because all three sides wanted his support. St. Jerome was a literary celebrity already, and he had retired to the desert to be alone with his meditations. Instead he was besieged by representatives of the three contending factions. Each one of them knew that, with Jerome on board, the victory was practically won.

But who could tell Jerome which faction really represented the holy Catholic Church? Only one man in the world: the pope. Whoever was in communion with Rome was the real bishop; the rest were impostors. The problem was that Pope Damasus hadn't made a definite decision yet. Antioch was in such a tangle that it was nearly impossible to untie the knot. So Jerome wrote a pleading letter to the pope, stuffing it with Scripture references. Jerome was a master of rhetoric, and he could flatter if he wanted to (though he was also the insult king of late antiquity). But one thing shines through in his letter: his sincere desire to cling to the chair of Peter. Only if he is sure he is on the pope's side can he be sure that he is standing with the real Christian Church. Thus he writes to Damasus:

By her importunity the widow in the gospel at last gained a hearing [see Matthew 15:28], and by the same means one friend induced another to give him bread at midnight, when his door was shut and his servants were in bed [Luke 11:7–8]. The publican's prayers overcame God [Luke 18:10–14], although God is invincible. Nineveh was saved by its tears from the impending ruin caused by its sin [Jonah 3:5, 10].

Why all these far-fetched references? you ask. For this reason, I answer: so that you in your greatness should look upon me in my littleness; that you, the rich shepherd, should not despise me, the ailing sheep. Christ Himself brought the robber from the cross to paradise [see Luke 23:43], and to show that repentance is never too late, he turned a murderer's death into a martyrdom. Gladly does Christ embrace the prodigal son when he returns to him [Luke 15:20], and leaving the ninety and nine, the good shepherd carries home on his shoulders the one poor sheep that is left [Luke 15:5].

From a persecutor Paul becomes a preacher. His bodily eyes are blinded to clear the eyes of his soul [Acts 9:8], and he who once hauled Christ's servants in chains before the council of the Jews [Acts 8:3] lives afterwards to glory in the bonds of Christ [2 Corinthians 12:10].

As I have already written to you, I, who have received Christ's garb in Rome, am now detained in the desert that borders Syria. No sentence of banishment, however, has been passed upon me; the punishment which I am undergoing is self-inflicted.

But, as the heathen poet says, "They change not mind but sky who cross the sea." The untiring foe follows me closely, and the assaults that I suffer in the desert are severer than ever. For the Arian frenzy raves, and the powers of the world support it. The church is torn apart into three factions, and each of these is eager to seize me for its own. The influence of the monks is of long standing, and it is directed against me. I meantime keep shouting, "He who clings to the chair of Peter is accepted by me."

Meletius, Vitalis, and Paulinus all profess to cleave to you, and I could believe the assertion if it were made by one of them only. As it is, either two of them or else all three are guilty of falsehood. Therefore I implore your blessedness, by our Lord's cross and passion, those necessary glories of our faith, as you hold an apostolic office, to give an apostolic decision. Only tell me by letter with whom I am to communicate in Syria, and I will pray for you that you may sit in judgment enthroned with the twelve [see Matthew 19:28]; that when you grow old, like Peter, you may be girded not by yourself but by another [John 21:18]; and that, like Paul, you may be made a citizen of the heavenly kingdom. Do not despise a soul for which Christ died.[33]

Because he refused to take sides, Jerome was called all sorts of names, which irked him, even in his wilderness hideaway. We can tell this from a letter he wrote to Marcus, a priest of some renown among the monks of the Chalcidian desert.

I am called a heretic, although I preach the consubstantial trinity. I am accused of the Sabellian impiety, although I proclaim with unwearied voice that in the Godhead there are three distinct, real, whole, and perfect persons. The Arians do right to accuse me, but the orthodox forfeit their orthodoxy when they assail a faith like mine. They may, if they like, condemn me as a heretic; but if they do they must also condemn Egypt and the West, Damasus and Peter. Why do they fasten the guilt on one and leave his companions uncensured? If there is but little water in the stream, it is the fault, not of the channel, but of the source.

I blush to say it, but from the caves which serve us for cells we monks of the desert condemn the world. Rolling in sack-cloth and ashes, we pass sentence on bishops. What use is the robe of a penitent if it covers the pride of a king? Chains, squalor, and long hair are by right tokens of sorrow, and not ensigns of royalty. I merely ask leave to remain silent. Why do they torment a man who does not deserve their ill-will?[34]

• • •

Damasus tried his best to bring clarity to the situation in Antioch. Theodoret preserves a letter the pope wrote to the Eastern bishops. As a piece of papal history, it's notable for its assumption of unquestioned authority.

Inasmuch as your love renders to the apostolic see the reverence which is its due, accept the same in no stingy measure for yourselves. For even though in the holy church in which the holy apostle sat, and taught us how it becomes us to manage the rudder which has been committed to us, we nevertheless confess ourselves to be unworthy of the honor, we yet on this very account strive by every means within our power to achieve, if possible, the glory of that blessedness.

Know then that we have condemned Timotheus, the unhallowed, the disciple of Apollinarius the heretic, together with his impious doctrine, and are confident that for the future his remains will have no weight whatever.

But if that old serpent, though smitten once and again, still revives to his own destruction, who though he exists outside the church never ceases from the attempt by his deadly venom to overthrow certain unfaithful men, do you avoid it as you would a pest, mindful ever of the apostolic faith—that, I mean, which was set out in writing by the Fathers at Nicaea; do you remain on steady ground, firm and unmoved in the faith, and henceforward allow neither your clergy nor laity to listen to vain words and futile questions, for we have already given a form, that he who professes himself a Christian may keep it, the form delivered by the Apostles, as says St. Paul, "if any one preach to you another gospel than that you have received let him be Anathema." For Christ the Son of God, our Lord, gave by his own passion abundant salvation to the race of men, that he might free from all sin the whole man involved in sin. If any one speaks of Christ as having had less of manhood or of Godhead, he is full of devils' spirits, and proclaims himself a child of hell.

Why then do you again ask me for the condemnation of Timotheus? Here, by the judgment of the apostolic see, in the presence of Peter, bishop of Alexandria, he was condemned, together with his teacher, Apollinarius, who will also in the day of judgment undergo due punishment and torment. But if he succeeds in persuading some less stable men, as though having some hope, after by his confession changing the true hope which is in Christ, with him shall likewise perish whoever of set purpose withstands the order of the Church. May God keep you sound, most honored sons.[35]

Theodoret also gives us "a confession of the Catholic faith which Pope Damasus sent to Bishop Paulinus in Macedonia when he was at Thessalonica." This again shows us the pope defining Christian doctrine with authority. For example:

We…anathematize those who do not with all freedom preach that the Holy Spirit is of one and the same substance and power with the Father and the Son. In like manner we anathematize those who follow the error of Sabellius and say that the Father and the Son are the same. We anathematize Arius and Eunomius, who with equal impiety, though with differences of phrase, maintain the Son and the Holy Spirit to be a creature. We anathematize the Macedonians who, produced from the root of Arius, have changed the name but not the impiety. We anathematize Photinus who, renewing the heresy of Ebion, confessed that our Lord Jesus Christ was only of Mary. We anathematize those who maintain that there are two sons—one before the ages and another after the assumption of the flesh from Mary. We anathematize also all who maintain that the Word of God moved in human flesh instead of a reasonable soul. For this Word of God Himself was not in His own body instead of a reasonable and intellectual soul, but assumed and saved our soul, both reasonable and intellectual, without sin. We anathematize also those who say that the Word of God is separated from the Father by extension and contraction, and blasphemously affirm that He is without essential being or is destined to die.[36]

And so on. Finally,

> This is the salvation of the Christians, that believing in the Trinity—that is, in the Father and the Son and the Holy Ghost—and being baptized into the same one Godhead and power and divinity and substance, in Him we may trust.[37]

· · ·

Not everyone submitted to Damasus's authority, of course. Some heretics defied him. But the worst were the ones who cheated. In an era of hand-copied manuscripts, the truths embodied in Scripture and in the Tradition of the Church could be falsified. We learn with some amazement that forgery was a common tool in theological controversy.

Rufinus tells us about one particularly devious attempt at forgery. It could be called reverse forgery, since it was a breathtakingly audacious attempt to make the true reading *look* like a forgery. The "certain friend" mentioned by Rufinus is St. Jerome.

> When a consultation was being held in the matter of the reconciling of the followers of Apollinarius to the church, Bishop Damasus wanted to have a document setting forth the faith of the church, which should be subscribed by those

who wished to be reconciled. The compiling of this document he entrusted to a certain friend of his, a priest and a highly accomplished man, who usually acted for him in matters of this kind. When he came to compose the document, he found it necessary, in speaking of the Incarnation of our Lord, to apply to him the expression *Homo Dominicus*. The Apollinarists took offense at this expression, and began to impugn it as a novelty. The writer of the document thereupon undertook to defend himself, and to confute the objectors by the authority of ancient Catholic writers; and he happened to show to one of those who complained of the novelty of the expression a book of the bishop Athanasius in which the word which was under discussion occurred. The man to whom this evidence was offered appeared to be convinced, and asked that the manuscript should be lent to him so that he might convince the rest who from their ignorance were still maintaining their objections.

When he had the manuscript in his hands, he devised a perfectly new method of falsification. He first erased the passage in which the expression occurred, and then wrote in again *the same words* he had erased! Then he returned the paper, and it was accepted without question.

The controversy about this expression again arose; the manuscript was brought forward. The expression in question was found in it, but in a position where something had been erased—and the man who had brought forward such a manuscript lost all authority, since the erasure seemed to be the proof of malpractice and falsification.

However,… it was a living man who was thus treated by a living man, and he at once did all in his power to lay bare the iniquitous fraud that had been committed, and to remove the stain of this nefarious act from the man who was innocent and had done no evil of the kind, and to attach it to the real author of the deed, so that it should completely overwhelm him with infamy.[38]

Jerome in turn wrote:

What nonsense is this out of which they fabricate a charge against me! It seems hardly worthwhile to notice it.…

I beg you, my dearest friend, that in these matters of serious interest to the church, where doctrinal truth is in question, and we are seeking for the authority of our predecessors for the well-being of our souls, to put away silly stuff of this kind, and not take mere after-dinner stories as if they were arguments.[39]

Heretics were commonly evasive about their teachings too, claiming to teach true Catholic doctrine while divulging a different "hidden truth" to their disciples, distorting the words of Christian teaching to mean something else. One of these heretics was Vitalius, who had submitted to Damasus an orthodox declaration of faith. Only later did Damasus discover that Vitalius was not teaching anything like what he had written in his declaration.

St. Gregory Nazianzen wrote of this:

But that they may not accuse us of having once accepted but of now repudiating the faith of their beloved Vitalius, which he handed in in writing at the request of the blessed Bishop Damasus of Rome, I will give a short explanation on this point also. For these men, when they are theologizing among their genuine disciples, and those who are initiated into their secrets, like the Manicheans among those whom they call the Elect, expose the full extent of their disease, and scarcely allow flesh at all to the Savior. But when they are refuted and pressed with the common answers about the Incarnation which the Scripture presents, they confess indeed the orthodox words, but they do violence to the sense; for they acknowledge the Manhood to be neither without soul nor without reason nor without mind, nor imperfect, but they bring in the Godhead to supply the soul and reason and mind, as though it had mingled itself only with Christ's flesh and not with the other properties belonging to us men, although his sinlessness was far above us and was the cleansing of our passions....

Since then these expressions, rightly understood, make for orthodoxy, but wrongly interpreted are heretical, what is there to be surprised at if we received the words of Vitalius in the more orthodox sense; our desire that they should be so meant persuading us, though others are angry at the intention of his writings? This is, I think, the reason why Damasus himself, having been subsequently better informed, and at the same time learning that they hold by their former explanations, excommunicated them and overturned their written confession of faith with an anathema; as well as because he was vexed at the deceit which he had suffered from them through simplicity.[40]

· · ·

What could be done about such slippery characters? The best thing was to have an accurate reading of Scripture, one that would settle all disputes. That wasn't as easy as it sounds. At a time when there was no printing, each copy of Scripture was unique. Copyists were especially careful with sacred texts, but errors still crept in.

There was also a language barrier, and a rather complicated one. By the time of Damasus, knowledge of Greek was growing rare in the West, even though it was the daily language of the whole Eastern half of the empire. The books of the New Testament were written in Greek originally, and Christians had long known the Old Testament from a Greek translation called the Septuagint (from the Greek for "seventy," after the ancient tradition that seventy translators worked on it). Most of the Old Testament was originally written in Hebrew, but very few Christians had any knowledge of Hebrew.

For the Latin-speaking West, it was vital to have a reliable translation of Scripture. There were translations of most of the books, made at different times and with varying degrees of accuracy and finesse, but there was no complete Latin Bible that could be relied on for establishing doctrine. The various translations, Damasus decided, needed to be sorted out, revised, and made accurate enough that there could be no doubt about what Scripture said. A standard Latin version would settle arguments and at least keep the heretics honest.

Jerome, who had always been Damasus's right-hand man in matters that required deep thought was clearly the man to do it. His was the assignment of revising the existing Latin translations and filling in the gaps. What he did with that assignment, however, was something much greater than what the pope had originally outlined.

The Christians of the time naturally looked to the Greek version of the Old Testament as their authority, and many believed it was as much divinely inspired as the Hebrew original. But Jerome, who could not do anything by halves, went straight back to the Hebrew and started translating from scratch. (He learned Hebrew from the best Jewish teachers he could find, and he learned it well enough that he taught the language to some of his friends.) Some parts of the older translations made it into Jerome's version if he thought they were accurate, but nothing was included that didn't match the Hebrew.

If you've been around for a while, you may remember how much uproar there was over replacing the familiar Douay Bible as the standard English translation for Catholics. And of course there are many Protestants today who sneer at any version that is not the *King James Bible*. That might give you some idea of how people reacted to news of Jerome's project. Jerome had to assure people that he meant no disparagement against the Septuagint.

The project took years, but when the Latin Bible was finally finished, it was a masterpiece. It soon became known as the "Vulgate" version, because it was in the "vulgar" tongue—that is, the language of the ordinary people of the West.

The historian Henry Hart Milman, an Anglican clergyman who was no fan of popery, beautifully summed up Jerome's achievement in the Vulgate.

> This was his great and indefeasible title to the appellation of a Father of the Latin Church. Whatever it may owe to the older and fragmentary versions of the sacred writings, Jerome's Bible is a wonderful work, still more as achieved by one man, and that a Western Christian, even with all the advantage of study and of residence in the East. It almost created a new language. The inflexible Latin became pliant and expansive, naturalizing foreign Eastern imagery, Eastern modes of expression and of

thought, and Eastern religious notions, most uncongenial to its own genius and character; and yet retaining much of its own peculiar strength, solidity, and majesty. If the Northern, the Teutonic languages, coalesce with greater facility with the Orientalism of the Scriptures, it is the triumph of Jerome to have brought the more dissonant Latin into harmony with the Eastern tongues. The Vulgate was even more, perhaps, than the Papal power the foundation of Latin Christianity.[41]

We should add that Jerome was the man with the literary genius, but it was Pope Damasus who saw the need to employ that genius. At a time when the intellectuals of the age were overheating their brains with abstruse theories, Damasus—who was a considerable intellectual himself—saw that, without a firm basis in Scripture, the teaching of the Church could far too easily run off the rails. Damasus's legacy is that firm basis in Scripture, which he gave us by setting one of the great literary minds of all time to the task.

CHAPTER FIVE

St. Leo the Great

(440–461)

T ents, horses, hundreds of thousands of soldiers, and all the barbaric splendor of a Hunnish camp cover the landscape as far as the eye can see. In the middle of it all stands one tent far more splendid than the rest and one barbarian far prouder. This is Attila, the so-called Scourge of God, who has humbled emperors and made cities vanish. He is now in Italy, and the imperial city of Rome is his next obvious target.

But today Attila is meeting the most formidable adversary he has ever faced. His generals scrutinize his face for any signs of his attitude. Is Attila unconcerned? Contemptuous? Wary? Terrified? It's impossible to say.

Here comes the enemy now, escorted through the camp by some of Attila's top men. The generals peer anxiously at the new arrival. He is unarmed; there are only a few old men in his party. Yet they feel instinctively that this one man outweighs the whole Hunnish horde behind them. For this is Leo, Bishop of Rome, leader of the Christian

Church, and perhaps—the generals won't rule out the possibility—bearer of the wrath of God.

. . .

Some popes are remembered for their exceptional holiness, or for their teaching, or for their courage in standing up to opposition. Only a few are remembered for all those things. History remembers exactly three popes, and possibly a fourth, as exceptional enough to attach the word *Great* to their names. Leo the Great is the first of them. (The others are Gregory I, Nicholas I, and possibly—it's too early to tell—John Paul II.)

Unlike "Blessed" or "Saint," "the Great" isn't an official designation made by the Catholic Church after a rigorous investigation. It's more of a democratic election. People started calling certain popes "the Great," and they kept it up for generations, until it was a permanent attachment to the popes' names.

Leo was not a perfect human being, of course—no pope is. But he was as close to the ideal as a human being can come. He administered the Church with faith, charity, and persistence. He defined important doctrines for all time. And he saved hundreds of thousands of people from the devastating wrath of the Huns.

If you asked Leo, he would probably tell you that the Monophysite heresy, not that pest Attila, was the biggest challenge of his reign.

The East had been swinging back and forth from one strange opinion to another for years. The Arians denied that the Son was equal to the Father; the Nestorians lurched in the other direction, completely separating Christ's human nature from his divine nature and denying that Mary could be called "Mother of God." Now the Monophysites were claiming that there were not two natures in Christ but only the one divine nature.

In all this yanking back and forth, the popes were doing their best to steer the straight and narrow course of orthodoxy. As we saw with Liberius, it wasn't always easy. One of the leaders of the Monophysite party was Eutyches. Leo felt compelled to strongly condemn his position.

If [Eutyches] did not know what he was bound to think concerning the incarnation of the Word of God, and he did not wish to gain the light of knowledge by researches through the length and breadth of the Holy Scriptures, he might at least have listened attentively to that general and uniform confession, in which the whole body of the faithful confess that they *believe in God the Father Almighty, and in Jesus Christ, His only Son, our Lord, who was born of the Holy Spirit and the Virgin Mary.*

By those three statements the devices of almost all heretics are overthrown. For not only is God believed to be both Almighty and the Father, but the Son is shown to be co-eternal with Him, differing in nothing from the Father because He is GOD from GOD, Almighty from Almighty, and being born from the Eternal one is co-eternal with Him; not later in point of time, not lower in power, not unlike in glory, not divided in essence: but at the same time the only begotten of the eternal Father was born eternal of the Holy Spirit and the Virgin Mary. And this nativity which took place in time took nothing from, and added nothing to that divine and eternal birth, but expended itself wholly on the restoration of man who had been deceived: in order that he might both vanquish death and overthrow by his strength the devil, who possessed the power of death. For we should not now be able to overcome the author of sin and death unless Christ took our nature on him and made it his own—Christ whom sin could not pollute and death could not hold. Doubtless then, he was conceived of the Holy Spirit within the womb of his Virgin Mother, who brought him forth without the loss of her virginity, even as she conceived him without its loss.

From here Leo goes on to define the orthodox Catholic doctrine—and to define it so precisely and clearly that his definition has been the basis for all statements of the doctrine since then.

Without detriment therefore to the properties of either nature and substance that came together in one person at that time, majesty took on humility, strength weakness, eternity mortality; and in order to pay off the debt belonging to our condition, inviolable nature was united with passible nature, so that, as suited the needs of our case, one and the same Mediator between God and men, the Man Christ Jesus, could both die with the one and not die with the other.

Thus in the whole and perfect nature of true man, true God was born, complete in what was his own, complete in what was ours. And by "ours" we mean what the Creator formed in us from the beginning and what he undertook to repair. For what the deceiver brought in, and what man committed when he had been deceived, had no trace in the Savior. Nor, because he shared our weaknesses, did he therefore share our faults. He took the form of a slave without stain of sin, increasing the human and not diminishing the divine—because that emptying of himself by which the Invisible made himself visible and, Creator and Lord of all things though he is, wished to be a mortal, was the bending down of pity, not the failing of power. Thus he who, while remaining in the form of God made man, was also made man in the form of a slave. For both natures retain their own proper character without loss: and as the form of God did not do away with the form of a slave, so the form of a slave did not impair the form of God.[42]

This is Leo's best possible statement of the truth of the Incarnation. If Eutyches still clings to his error, it will be from stubbornness, not from ignorance.

We can see that Leo was a bit annoyed by what Eutyches had said; this comes through in the first part of the letter, where he faults Eutyches for not learning his Creed well enough. Further, Leo might have been annoyed by Eutyches's stubbornness, and he might have thought Eutyches's opinions were very dangerous. But that did not make Leo forget what it meant to be a Christian. If Eutyches came to his senses and gave up his misguided opinions, that should be the end of the whole ugly incident. There was no need to hold a grudge: Leo would not fault the bishops for taking Eutyches back into communion right away.

And yet, if he grieves over it faithfully and to good purpose, and, no matter how late it is, acknowledges how rightly the bishops' authority has been set in motion; or if with his own mouth and hand in your presence he recants his wrong opinions, then no mercy that is shown to him when he is penitent can be found fault with. Our Lord, that true and good Shepherd who laid down his life for his sheep and who came to save, not lose, our souls [John 10:11], wishes us to imitate his kindness, so that, while justice constrains us when we sin, mercy may prevent us from being rejected when we have returned.

In the end, the true faith is most profitably defended when a false belief is condemned even by its supporters.[43]

. . .

As for the fateful meeting between Leo and the great Hun, our sources are meager. One historian, however, gives a fairly thorough account of the events that surrounded it. Jordanes's *History of the Goths* is a summary of a larger history, now lost, by the famous Cassiodorus, who was a high official at the court of the Gothic king of Italy. (Much later in his very long life, Cassiodorus would found the Vivarium, a monastery where he literally saved Western civilization by setting his monks to work copying every manuscript they could get their hands on.)

Though Cassiodorus's account was written about eighty years after the events, most of the records of these events were easily available to someone with his connections. We have good reason to hope that his version of what happened is fairly accurate.

Jordanes tells us how Attila descended on Italy from the northeast.

> As his first move he besieged the city of Aquileia, the metropolis of Venetia, which is situated on a point or tongue of land by the Adriatic Sea. On the eastern side its walls are washed by the river Natissa, flowing from Mount Piccis. The siege was long and fierce, but of no avail, since the bravest soldiers of the Romans withstood him from within. At last his army was discontented and eager to withdraw.
>
> Attila happened to be walking around the walls, considering whether to break camp or delay longer, and noticed that the

white birds—namely, the storks—who build their nests in the gables of houses were bearing their young from the city and, contrary to their custom, were carrying them out into the country.

Since he was a shrewd observer of events, he understood this and said to his soldiers: "You see the birds foresee the future. They are leaving the city sure to perish and are forsaking strongholds doomed to fall by reason of imminent peril. Do not think this a meaningless or uncertain sign; fear, arising from the things they foresee, has changed their custom."

Why say more? He inflamed the hearts of his soldiers to attack Aquileia again. Constructing battering rams and bringing to bear all manner of engines of war, they quickly forced their way into the city, laid it waste, divided the spoil and so cruelly devastated it as scarcely to leave a trace to be seen.[44]

Here we see a side of Attila's character that may be very important to the story of his encounter with Leo. Superstition was probably more the rule than the exception among both Romans and barbarians (you'll notice that Jordanes unquestioningly accepts Attila's conclusion as obviously correct), but Attila seems to have been unusually superstitious even for his time. In this case his superstition leads him to success.

Incidentally, the destruction of Aquileia had a profound effect on Italian history. Refugees from Attila's attacks, and from the ravages of innumerable other barbarians who used Venetia as the highway to Italy, moved to easily defended marshy islands in the lagoon. As more and more refugees flooded in, a city started to grow there, so that today the metropolis of Venetia is not Aquileia but the watery city of Venice.

After they had destroyed Aquileia, Attila's Huns seemed like an unstoppable tidal wave of destruction.

> Then growing bolder and still thirsting for Roman blood, the Huns raged madly through the remaining cities of Venetia. They also laid waste Milan, the metropolis of Liguria, once an imperial city, and gave over Ticinum [now Pavia] to a like fate. Then they destroyed the neighboring country in their frenzy and demolished almost the whole of Italy.[45]

The destruction of Milan was a bigger deal than this terse narrative might make us think. Milan had surpassed Rome as the largest city in Italy, and it had been the imperial capital (the emperors having largely lost interest in Rome itself). The destruction of Milan would have struck the people of Rome the same way it would strike people in Washington, D.C., if New York City were not simply attacked but wiped completely off the map.

From Milan, of course, Rome was the next obvious target. But Jordanes tells us that superstition was this time at work in Rome's defense.

> Attila's mind had been bent on going to Rome. But his followers, as the historian Priscus relates, took him away, not out of regard for the city to which they were hostile but because they remembered the case of Alaric, the former king of the Visigoths. They distrusted the good fortune of their own king, inasmuch as Alaric did not live long after the sack of Rome, but straightway departed this life.[46]

Forty years earlier Alaric had sacked Rome, which had not seen a foreign invader for eight hundred years. But he died of a fever almost immediately after that.

While Attila's spirit was wavering in doubt between going and not going, and he was still waiting around to think it over, an embassy came to him from Rome to seek peace. Pope Leo himself came to meet him in the Ambuleian district of the Veneti at the well-traveled ford of the river Mincius. Then Attila quickly put aside his usual fury, turned back on the way he had advanced from beyond the Danube, and departed with the promise of peace.[47]

Jordanes maddeningly leaves out the details of the famous meeting between Leo and Attila. Perhaps Leo had some idea about Attila's superstitious nature and so emphasized the terrible fate of Alaric. Attila was a pagan who probably believed in different gods for different nations. The Christian God might have seemed a real force protecting his holy city of Rome and taking a terrible revenge on her enemies. And the spectacle of an unarmed bishop who had the courage to come and confront the terror of the civilized world must have made an impression on him.

We too stand amazed at the courage of Leo. Attila was a holy terror if ever there was one, and the Huns were known for their creativity in coming up with cruel tortures for their captives. Yet Leo went out to meet this unstoppable force of nature with quiet confidence.

Not long after that meeting, Attila died in his sleep. One account says he died of a nosebleed after drinking excessively in celebration of his latest marriage; another says he was stabbed by his new Gothic wife. Some modern historians think he may have been assassinated by Roman agents. At any rate, it was an inglorious end for the great conqueror who had fought a thousand battles and destroyed countless cities.

This story of the meeting of Attila and Leo, barbarism and civilization, raw violence and the power of faith, has fascinated readers and writers for centuries. The story shows what the pope had become by this time. Emperors cowered before the rage of the unstoppable barbarian, but Attila could not make Leo cower. The world could see that this man stood at the head of the whole Church. And the Church had been so successful in its first four centuries—a success that seemed so obviously supernatural—that one of the most feared and ruthless conquerors who ever lived thought he'd better do what the pope asked.

CHAPTER SIX

Vigilius
(537–555)

*I*n the Basilica of St. Peter in Constantinople, a tall, fat, and unarmed old man clings desperately to the columns of the altar. Soldiers surround him, with enough weapons to put down an army of rioters. They demand that he come with them, but the old man refuses to leave the altar.

While helpless deacons watch in horror, the soldiers suddenly grab the man by whatever they can reach—hair, legs, beard, robes—and try to carry him away. He clings more tightly to the columns until one of them cracks, and the huge stone altar threatens to fall on him. The deacons rush in to hold it up.

The soldiers give up and leave the church. Perhaps they're tired. Or perhaps they've been struck by horror at what nearly happened. They may be wondering how they would explain to the people of the city that they had killed their pope.

So Pope Vigilius lives another day. But there may well be times when he'll wish he had been crushed by that altar. There will certainly be days when he wishes he had never become pope.

But it's his own fault. No one ever worked harder to become pope than Vigilius did.

• • •

It might seem strange to an outsider, but no matter how powerful the popes became, either as spiritual leaders or worldly rulers, only Peter was able to choose his successor. In the year 532 Boniface II tried to break that tradition. His nominee was a deacon named Vigilius, a portly aristocrat who was rich and well educated, a friend of all the best families in Rome. Why Boniface thought Vigilius was qualified to be pope is anybody's guess, but to judge by Vigilius's future, there could have been money involved.

At any rate, Boniface failed. The people of Rome, who traditionally elected the pope, were so outraged—probably riotously so—that Boniface not only revoked but even burned his own decree. No doubt that was a bitter disappointment to Vigilius.

But if Vigilius had one virtue, it was that he didn't give up easily. He kept looking for his opportunity.

These were strange and perilous times. The whole world seemed to be in an uproar, and the city of Rome was facing the worst dangers in its history. In the year 476 the last of the Roman emperors of the West had resigned. He was a young boy named Romulus, called "Augustulus" or "little Augustus" by his contemptuous subjects. For some time the so-called emperor had been a puppet in the hands of some barbarian general or other, and the latest barbarian kingmaker had decided that he could do without a puppet.

There was still a Roman emperor, but he lived in Constantinople (which we now call Istanbul). Rome itself was no longer part of the Roman Empire. Instead barbarian kings—first Odoacer and then the Gothic Theodoric the Great—ruled Italy, supposedly in the name of the emperor but only in the way that the Canadian government rules in the name of the queen of England, without expecting her to exercise any real power.

After half a century of this barbarian rule, a new emperor came to the throne in Constantinople—an ambitious man who conceived the almost absurd notion of reconquering the whole Western Empire. His name was Justinian, and he almost succeeded. His brilliant general Belisarius reconquered the old province of Africa (roughly modern Tunisia and Algeria), including the great city of Carthage. Then he set his sights on the real prize: Italy and, above all, Rome herself.

It took years of devastating war to reconquer Italy. The Romans at first welcomed the imperial government, but it wasn't long before they had plenty of reason to regret their enthusiasm. When the war began Rome was still great among the cities of the earth, with an enormous population, gushing fountains and public baths, glorious architecture, and a thriving literary culture. By the end of the war the place was a grubby and depopulated ruin.

And the imperial government rapidly proved itself a far worse plague than the barbarian rulers had ever been. The tax gatherers had to have their taxes. If barbarians killed your neighbors, that meant that you owed their taxes as well as your own. If you said you couldn't pay, there were all kinds of tortures that were very effective in helping you remember where you might have hidden a few coins.

• • •

In the middle of all this turmoil came the Monophysite heresy. Orthodox Catholic Christians believe that Christ has both a human and a divine nature; Monophysites (from Greek meaning "one nature") believed that Christ had only a divine nature. The empress Theodora, a former chorus girl who had been lucky enough to marry Justinian, had fallen in with that sect, and she quickly became a fanatic. She did everything in her power—and in many ways she had more power than Justinian—to promote her Monophysite pets, and her dearest wish was to see Monophysites triumph over the orthodox.

The now-reigning Pope Silverius happened to send the deacon Vigilius to Constantinople as his representative. There Vigilius got to know Theodora. Vigilius still had ambitions, and the papacy was his obvious target. A man should be able to live quite comfortably as pope, with as much power as any citizen below the emperor and as much wealth as he could spend.

The Roman populace was of course poisoned against Vigilius because of his earlier attempt at the office. But who in the empire had the power to overrule even the Roman mob? Theodora.

Vigilius made the empress a sensible offer. Make me the pope, he said, and I'll fall in with your Monophysite program. Some say he also offered her two hundred pounds of gold—an enormous bribe.

This was too good for Theodora to pass up.

The empress had already tried to get Pope Silverius to see things her way, but he was stubborn. "Now I know this woman is planning to kill me," he had told his friends after refusing one of Theodora's polite requests. Now by merely bullying a few people, which was what Theodora did all day long anyway, she could get a pope from her side into office. Vigilius was shipped back to Rome with letters for Belisarius that made it quite clear what Theodora wanted.

There were difficulties, of course. One would be to get rid of the current pope. Also, Rome was under imperial authority but only barely. Justinian's brilliant general was still in the middle of taking Italy back from the Goths.

Belisarius had been so successful in taking back Africa that the Goths were scared half to death of him. As he marched toward Rome, the

Gothic armies took refuge in the fortress city of Ravenna. The Romans welcomed Belisarius as the long-awaited restorer of the empire in the West. But then the Goths got their act together, came down from Ravenna, and besieged Rome.

This is when the splendor of ancient Rome was destroyed. Masterpieces of sculpture that had stood for centuries became mere ammunition to hurl at the Goths in desperate battles. Famous buildings were battered and broken. The Goths cut the aqueducts, and the fountains of Rome stopped flowing, not to flow again for almost a thousand years.

This was the scene when Vigilius came back with his letters from Constantinople. These letters to Belisarius were explicit: He was to get rid of Pope Silverius by any means necessary.

Belisarius knew firsthand that if Theodora wanted something, she would get it one way or another. The only question was how many people she would have to sweep out of the way first. Would Belisarius be swept, or would he do the sweeping?

It was easy enough to get rid of Silverius. A letter suddenly appeared in which Silverius offered to open the gates of the city to the Gothic army. Treason! Silverius said the letter was a forgery, but he was overruled and deposed. Belisarius ensured that Vigilius was elected to replace him.

The first thing Vigilius did was to have the deposed Pope Silverius handed over to his own protective care. Silverius didn't survive long: The *Liber Pontificalis* says that Vigilius "sent him into exile in Pontiae and fed him with the bread of tribulation and the water of bitterness. And he fell ill and died a confessor."[48]

· · ·

Now that Vigilius was secure in his throne—or as secure as anyone could be with Italy in its miserable state of constant war—the next obvious step would be to recall all the Monophysite bishops who had been deprived of their sees because of their heresy. But something strange happened to Vigilius. Now that he was pope, he gradually lost interest in the Monophysites. In fact, he seemed to turn quite orthodox in a few years.

Theodora waited, but there was no change in Rome's attitude toward the Monophysites. Eventually she wrote Vigilius a little letter. Here is how the *Liber Pontificalis*, from which much of our meager information about Vigilius comes, tells the story:

Then Theodora Augusta wrote to Pope Vigilius: "Come, fulfill for us what you promised of your own free will concerning our father Anthemius [or Anthimus, a prominent Monophysite bishop] and restore him to office."

But Vigilius replied: "Far be this from me, Lady Augusta. Earlier I spoke wrong and foolishly. Now I absolutely refuse to restore a man who is a heretic and under the anathema. Though I am unworthy, I am the vicar of blessed Peter, the apostle, as were my predecessors, the most holy Agapitus and Silverius, who condemned him."[49]

We can imagine how Theodora would have received this reply. What confounded insolence! Didn't they have an agreement? If she had known Vigilius was going to do *this* with the papacy, she never would have sold it to him! And what's this about "the most holy Silverius"? Didn't Vigilius see to it that Silverius had "the bread of tribulation and the water of bitterness" stuffed down his throat until he died?

We have a harder time imagining what might have been going through Vigilius's mind. He knew what Theodora was capable of; he had seen how easy it was for her to get rid of Silverius. And all he had wanted was a cushy job. Then why this sudden courage in doctrine?

What made Vigilius stand up to one of the cruelest and most ruthless rulers in history? It seems almost supernatural.

Certainly Vigilius didn't display an abundance of other virtues. When Theodora decided it was time for revenge, there was no shortage of charges to bring against Vigilius, supported by the testimony of ordinary Romans. Messengers came to Constantinople accusing Vigilius, who apparently had a hot temper, of the worst possible crimes.

> We declare him to be a murderer. For he abandoned himself to rage and struck his notary so hard that he fell right down and died. And he gave his niece Vigilia to the consul Asterius, son of a widow woman; then, on some pretext, he had Asterius arrested in the middle of the night and beaten until he died.[50]

Theodora put her representative on a ship to Rome with orders to arrest Vigilius. "If you find him in St. Peter's," she told him, "leave him alone. But if you find him in the Lateran or in the palace or in any other church, stick him on a ship right away and send him to me—or by God I'll have you skinned alive."[51] Theodora had really fine-tuned the art of motivation.

Vigilius was arrested in the Church of St. Cecilia. We get the impression that he may have created quite a climate of fear among the citizens of Rome. Or perhaps he was a divisive figure, with fans among the aristocracy and mortal enemies among the common people. While the imperial ship was waiting to depart, the crowds seemed to be watching their bishop's arrest sadly, begging him to say a prayer for them, as if he were a martyr on his way to glory. But as soon as the ship started to move away from the dock, a change came over the crowd.

"Good riddance!" people shouted. "And take your famine and your plague with you!" They threw sticks and stones and dirty old pots at him. "You've done evil to the Romans—we hope evil follows you wherever you go!"[52]

Vigilius was taken to Sicily, which was a reliable imperial stronghold, and he seems to have been treated with courtesy and allowed to keep his wealth. In spite of the insults at his departure, he managed to send a fleet of ships filled with grain to the starving people of Rome.

Vigilius stayed in Sicily for some time. When at last he reached Constantinople, the emperor treated him as an honored guest rather than as a prisoner.

• • •

Justinian had his private reasons for wanting to be on the pope's good side. Not satisfied with being emperor of the world, he had decided to turn theologian and settle this Monophysite controversy once and for all. The Council of Chalcedon was supposed to have settled it, but the Monophysites refused to recognize that council.

Minutely examining the writings of three Syrian bishops, all of them dead, Justinian found heresies in them that had to be condemned— even though the three bishops had been participants in the Council of Chalcedon. These "Three Chapters," he believed, tended toward the heresy of Nestorianism, the opposite of Monophysitism. (Justinian wasn't altogether wrong about that.) By condemning them, Justinian thought, he would remove all reasonable grounds for the Monophysites' objections. Certain writings of two of these bishops were to be placed under anathema; but the bishop whom Justinian considered the worst offender, Theodore of Mopsuestia, had to be condemned personally as well, even though he had died in communion with the Church.

"Therefore," the emperor concluded, "if after this true confession of faith and condemnation of the heretics, anyone separates himself from the holy Church of God because of words and syllables and trivial arguments about phrases—as if religion were a matter of terms and ways of speaking rather than deeds—then that person will have to answer for his love of division."[53]

But of course it wasn't that easy. The Monophysites weren't satisfied at all, and now the orthodox Catholics were up in arms. Was the emperor presuming to judge or revise the holy Council of Chalcedon?

In the Greek-speaking East, where the emperor could easily make heads roll whenever he wanted, the bishops mostly subscribed to Justinian's pronouncement and condemned the "Three Chapters"— though the patriarch of Constantinople made it clear that his assent was conditional, and he would withdraw it if the pope didn't agree. But in the Latin-speaking West, most of the clergy circled the wagons and prepared to defend the Council of Chalcedon against the meddling emperor.

In these circumstances the pope's opinion would obviously make a big difference, so Justinian showed Vigilius every honor when he arrived. But Vigilius immediately condemned all the Eastern bishops who had subscribed to Justinian's edict; he subjected them to four months of excommunication. He may even have gone so far as to excommunicate Theodora.

What had gotten into Vigilius? Had he grown a spine suddenly?

Perhaps politics was a good part of it: Theodora and Justinian were formidable opponents, but so was the Roman mob. Vigilius would have remembered his first attempt at the papacy and how the mob had forced Boniface to burn his edict making Vigilius his successor. Since the mob in Rome was fiercely orthodox, caving in to pressure in Constantinople could be a fatal mistake.

On the other hand, it may be that Vigilius had grown a conscience. After all, Rome was far away. If the people of Rome threw him out for giving in to Justinian, he could live the rest of his life in luxury in Constantinople.

Whatever had gotten into Vigilius, it wasn't permanent. He began to waver.

Part of the problem may have been language. The controversy about the Three Chapters depended on subtle theological arguments written in Greek. There had been a time when every educated Roman knew Greek, but that time was long past. Now very few Latin speakers were competent in Greek. And on the other hand, Latin was dying out in the East; Justinian would be the last Latin-speaking emperor in Constantinople. The two sides were arguing without really understanding each other very well.

Justinian did not have much patience for a long, drawn-out argument in which he was not getting his way. He used every art to persuade or bully Vigilius into condemning the Three Chapters and recalling the Monophysite bishops who had been deprived of their sees. After a few months Vigilius issued a judgment: Justinian was right about the Three Chapters. Not that there had been anything wrong with Chalcedon: Cursed be anyone who condemned that holy council.

The Western bishops were appalled: Vigilius had betrayed them! There was open rebellion against the pope in the West and even among the Latin bishops who had come to Constantinople. In the province of Africa, a local council formally excommunicated the pope.

The only way out, apparently, was for Vigilius to withdraw his judgment, flipping back to his original flop. Justinian allowed him to do it, seeing that even he and the pope couldn't keep a lid on the ecclesiastical rebellion. He extracted a promise from Vigilius that he would do all he could to bring the West around to Justinian's way of thinking eventually. Meanwhile, a general council of the Church should come together and decide the matter once and for all.

But Justinian couldn't resist bullying the council by firing bishops who refused to agree with him. The Eastern bishops who were left were willing to condemn the Three Chapters; the Western bishops were appalled by Justinian's interference and refused to budge. Condemnations and counter-condemnations ensued. Eventually Vigilius and twelve other Western bishops who were in Constantinople at the time condemned the patriarch of Constantinople himself for taking Justinian's side.

Justinian had finally had enough. He was so furious that the Western bishops decided it would be prudent to run for their lives. Vigilius decided to run to the Basilica of St. Peter—and that's where we met him at the beginning of this story.

• • •

Since Vigilius could not be extracted from his sanctuary without more violence than even Justinian was willing to sanction, the emperor tried persuasion. He sent Vigilius's old friend Belisarius to persuade the pope that no harm would come to him if he came out of the church. A parade of distinguished gentlemen of the court promised Vigilius safety if he came willingly and violence if he did not. Finally Vigilius accepted this oath of the court officials and went back with them to the imperial palace. But here he did not feel very safe: He was kept under armed guard, and all his followers were taunted in the streets. In the middle of the night, he slipped away to Chalcedon, a few miles from Constantinople.

Finally the promised council got under way. Justinian wanted Vigilius to preside, but he refused. All the Latin bishops stayed away; only Eastern bishops showed up. Vigilius wrote a treatise for the council, complaining that, while some of the writings Justinian had condemned were in fact wrong, the whole procedure of condemning them had been worse, and there was no precedent for anathematizing a man who had died in the peace of the Church.

The council responded by excommunicating Vigilius and sentencing him to be banished.

Already exiled from Rome, Vigilius was now tossed out of all civilization, plunked down on a little island in the Sea of Marmara. There he was left to wallow in his misery, which was made much more miserable by agonizing attacks of gout. Six months of that wallowing were enough to bend him. Vigilius wrote to the patriarch of Constantinople that he was now ready to agree with Justinian on every point.

After eight years of almost constant misery in Constantinople, Vigilius was finally allowed to return to Rome, which was now a broken shell of a city. But he never made it back. He stopped in Sicily again, and there, worn down by all his troubles, he died.

All Vigilius ever wanted was a cushy desk job. Was it his fault that he was born in a troubled time, when the only cushy desk jobs were in the Church? And instead of an easy life in a palace with all the good meals he wanted, he suffered torture and anxiety to defend the faith. Had he asked to be chosen to defend the faith? Did he pray for a martyr's life?

Vigilius was no hero. In fact, he was in almost every way a rotten pope: greedy, ill-tempered, cowardly, and devious. The best we can say for him is that he wasn't all bad, and the worst charges against him may have been exaggerated.

Yet he saved the Catholic faith. At a time when the strongest and most dedicated Christians were pulling in different directions and tearing the Church apart, Vigilius's waffling was probably what pushed the eventual result into a middle course. Justinian won his little theological battle but found it necessary to acknowledge (at least implicitly) that the pope, not the emperor, was the legitimate authority in the Church. Vigilius was compelled to admit that the writings Justinian had condemned had actually been wrong. The whole thing was agonizingly drawn-out and painful, but the Monophysite heresy did not win, Theodora's pet heretics were not reinstated, and Catholic orthodoxy prevailed.

If Vigilius had been a good man, we might have said he was a hero to steer the Church safely through such troubled waters. Since he was what he was, we can only say it was a miracle.

CHAPTER SEVEN

Benedict IX

(1032–1045)

"*H*is life after he became a priest was so foul, so loathsome, so horrible, that I shudder to speak of it."[54]

Not very often does one pope speak of another in those terms, but that was how Pope Victor III described Benedict IX, who had reigned during his lifetime. In fact, Benedict IX had been pope three times. No one else has ever been pope more than once. No other pope has ever sold the papacy either; Benedict IX managed that trick too. And while he was pope, he filled his time with orgies and dissipation.

"He was a disgrace to the chair of Peter," says the old *Catholic Encyclopedia*, and probably not a single historian would disagree with that assessment.[55]

• • •

Benedict—whose original name was Theophylact—was very young when he became pope. Some historians have said that he was only twelve years old, but twenty seems to be a more accurate figure: old enough that he already had a bit of misspent youth behind him when he began his misspent papacy.

It's hard for us to imagine a pope so young these days, but that's because the way of electing popes has changed. In 1032, when Theophylact became pope, the centuries-old rule was that the pope was chosen by the clergy and the people of Rome. There was no set mechanism by which the people made their choice—no papal ballot boxes or online polls. Sometimes the mob practically kidnapped a popular clergyman—not as bad a method as you might think, since it earned us, among others, Gregory the Great. But by the eleventh century, "the people" meant, for all practical purposes, the powerful and frequently feuding aristocratic families of the city.

One of Theophylact's uncles was Pope Benedict VIII. That pope was succeeded by another one of Theophylact's uncles, Pope John XIX. When this Uncle Pope died, Theophylact's father, Alberic, seems to have felt that the papacy belonged to the family—and he was powerful enough that, for the moment, no one could tell him otherwise.

Being pope would be a good career move for his younger son. Certainly Theophylact wasn't going to do anything useful on his own. His older and apparently more talented brother became the patrician, or secular governor, of Rome and in fact even took the ancient title of consul. The papacy seems to have been the answer to Alberic's question of what to do with a wastrel younger son who would never amount to anything. It cost Alberic a lot of money, but he probably considered it money well spent.

We don't know much about how Benedict IX fared as pope. There are some official acts in his name, but it's really impossible to tell whether he had much to do with them or whether the Roman ecclesiastical bureaucracy functioned in spite of him.

History tells us more about Benedict's personal life. It's not a pretty story. With all the money he could want at his disposal, the college-age pope turned his life into one big party. We don't know all the details of his recreations; many writers of the time were so horrified that they refused to say much about them. Other contemporaries mention adultery, rape, and murder as some of his hobbies. Some historians believe that he was mostly homosexual, although not exclusively, to judge by the complaints made by aristocratic husbands in Rome.

In Benedict's defense we should remember that his fortunes were bound up with the constant aristocratic family feuds of the time. His enemies could have exaggerated some of the horrors.

• • •

After less than four years on the throne of Peter, the young pope was run out of town. There was an assassination attempt by his family's enemies, right in the Basilica of St. Peter. We don't know how much popular support this uprising had; it may have been something like a riot, but it probably had more to do with the incessant feuds between the noble families of Rome than with the will of the common people.

Benedict was still pope, even in exile, and the next year (1037) he met the Holy Roman Emperor, who was technically the secular ruler of Italy and who was engaged in a massive military campaign to make that rule more than a technicality. The emperor gave Benedict his support, and that was enough to frighten Benedict's enemies. He came back to Rome.

Exile had not reformed the pope. He seems to have resumed his constant partying as soon as he was back in Rome, and he probably took every opportunity for revenge on his enemies. He did nothing to make himself popular. In 1044 he was thrown out again, probably by another aristocratic conspiracy.

Immediately Rome erupted in all-out civil war. The main part of Rome had turned against Benedict, but the Trastevere, the part of the city on the far side of the Tiber, was loyal to the exiled pope. Factions from the two sides fought a pitched battle in the beginning of 1045, and the victory went to the Trastevere. But the anti-Benedict party, two weeks after their defeat, sold the papacy to a man who began to call himself Pope Sylvester III.

From his country house in the hills, Benedict issued a furious excommunication against Sylvester. Sylvester laughed it off, so Benedict took the more practical measure of sending his family's private army to attack Rome. After a successful battle, the army threw Sylvester out and reinstalled Benedict. Thus began what most historians count as Benedict's second papacy.

But the papacy was beginning to lose its luster for Benedict. He was tired of having to pretend to be good, even if only just barely. But what really pushed him over the edge was falling in love: He wanted to marry his cousin. Even his own faction seemed to balk at the idea of a pope actually marrying (as opposed to merely raping and murdering), so Benedict thought he might resign.

Could a pope resign? Benedict went to John Gratian, a clergyman with a reputation for honesty and virtue who was also Benedict's godfather, to discuss the problem. His godfather convinced him that it was indeed possible for a pope to give up the rule of the Church. So Benedict came up with a brilliant suggestion. If John would give him a thousand pounds of gold (a prodigiously enormous sum), Benedict would resign, and John could be pope after him.

Thus, in 1045, Benedict cheerfully sold the papacy to John Gratian and went off to his country house to resume his orgies. John took the name Gregory VI and was hailed as the new pope by the clergy and people, who seem to have been glad to see the back of Benedict.

• • •

By all accounts Gregory VI was an unusually honest and virtuous man, although some of his contemporaries hint that he was not too bright. He probably thought he was doing the Church a favor—not so much buying the papacy as paving a golden highway to get the dreadful Benedict IX out of town. Nearly everyone was delighted to have a pope with a spotless reputation. Congratulations came in from everywhere.

Unfortunately for Gregory, it wasn't easy being pope. Sylvester III was still around and claiming the papal throne. What was far worse was that Benedict's cousin decided she didn't want to marry him after all. And if Benedict couldn't marry his cousin, then why had he given up the papacy? He decided he wanted to be pope again—and he still had his powerful family with its own private army.

Against these odds Gregory VI did his best to reform the papacy. Wherever he found virtue and talent (two things that were hard to find in Rome in those days), he encouraged them. In particular, he took in a young monk named Hildebrand, who seemed to be just the sort of virtuous and capable man the Church needed. Hildebrand supplied the brains that may have been lacking in Gregory VI, and the two of them made a first-rate team. But Gregory could never wipe away the stain of his transaction with Benedict. When he tried to implement vigorous reforms, his enemies accused him of simony.

The city was divided into three factions, one for each of the three men who claimed to be pope, and there were constant riots in the streets. Faced with this impossible situation, some of the few more or less neutral people of Rome—clergy and lay—sent a representative to King Henry III of Germany, son of the late Holy Roman Emperor and soon to be elected emperor himself, begging him to sort out the mess. Henry was glad to oblige, and incidentally to reaffirm his power as ruler of Italy.

Henry summoned all three popes to a synod that was to decide what to do with them, but it was apparent to everyone that Henry had already decided that none of them could be pope. Gregory presided and told the synod that, in buying the papacy from Benedict IX, he had been hoping to restore the power of electing the pope to the clergy and people, taking it out of the hands of the ever-feuding gangs of aristocrats. But the bishops at the synod politely suggested that the devil was very good at coming up with rationalizations like that, and Gregory—honest to the end—had to agree.

Gregory pronounced his own sentence: "I, Gregory, bishop, servant of the servants of God, because of the simony which, by the cunning of the devil, entered into my election, decide that I must be deposed from the Roman bishopric."[56]

Sylvester III was then stripped of all his ecclesiastical dignities and packed away to a monastery, while Benedict IX was officially deposed. There had been three popes; now there was no pope at all.

Henry put forward a German bishop as a candidate for the office, and the clergy were glad to accept, probably because Henry could be very persuasive when he put his mind to it. So Clement II, another very good and honest bishop, came to the papal throne. It looked as though things might settle down for a while.

Unfortunately, Rome was notoriously hard on northern constitutions. The grubby medieval city—so much decayed from the days when she was mistress of the world—was filled with fevers. Clement was installed as pope in 1046; in 1047 he died. Some of his contemporaries suspected that he had been poisoned, but it seems more likely that he just died of the usual Roman diseases.

News reached Henry in Germany that the pope had died, and Henry immediately proposed another nominee for the office. But more news came from Rome: Benedict was back.

• • •

After the synod that had deposed all three popes, Benedict IX had moved back to his pleasant country house, where he was surrounded by the immeasurable wealth of his family. As soon as he heard that the new pope was dead, Benedict put that wealth to good use. He spread gold around so lavishly that he was suddenly the most popular man in Rome. For about eight months he was pope again—his third papacy.

King Henry was furious. The secular authorities in Rome had been bought off. Boniface, the powerful Marquis of Tuscany, supported Benedict. He told Henry's candidate for the papal throne that a mere marquis could not oppose the will of the Romans.

Henry was not the sort of man to take that lying down. He wrote to Boniface: "Now, listen here. You've restored a pope who was canonically deposed, and your greed for gold has made you despise my commands. Well, if you don't change your ways, I'll come down there and make you."[57]

Henry meant it: He would definitely come with an army, and it would not be a good time for anyone who had defied him. Benedict was out, for the last time, and Henry's candidate was installed as Pope Damasus II.

Less than a month later, Pope Damasus was dead, struck down by another Roman fever (or poisoned by one of Benedict's friends, if you believe the most malicious rumors). Again, northerners didn't last long in Rome in those days.

• • •

We don't really know what happened to Benedict after his last expulsion from Rome. Some historians say he continued to claim that he was the real pope until he died. Others say he reformed and lived a quiet life. But there is a very strange story told by St. Peter Damian about a friend of a friend.

Once—we imagine it must have been a dark and stormy night—this friend of a friend was out riding, when suddenly he came around a corner, and there was a most hideous monster standing in his way. It looked something like an enormous bear, but it had the ears and the tail of a donkey.

Naturally the rider was terrified. But then the monster spoke.

"Don't be afraid," the hideous creature said. "Once I was a man like you. But because I lived like a beast, I have been forced to take the shape of a beast."

"But who were you?" the quivering rider asked.

"I am Benedict," the apparition replied, "the one who took the Apostolic See unworthily. Ever since I died, and till doomsday, I must be dragged through places of unspeakable horror filled with the stench of brimstone. When the Day of Judgment comes, I will be buried, body and soul, in the bottomless pit. There is no hope for me."[58]

There is a more cheerful, and probably more plausible, story about the end of Benedict. According to an abbot of Grottaferrata monastery, Benedict finally came to his senses and longed to make things right, or at least less egregiously wrong. He came to Grottaferrata and asked the abbot what he should do. The abbot told him in no uncertain terms that he must resign his bishopric and devote the rest of his life to penance. And Benedict became plain old Theophylact again and retired to private life.

• • •

Now, in all this sordid tale of the man who was pope three times, you may have noticed that we haven't heard anything about Christian doctrine, or at least not very much. That's because Benedict IX had no effect whatsoever on Christian doctrine. He was much too busy being rotten to worry about theology.

Is there a moral to the depressing story of Benedict IX?

Sometimes absolute rottenness can be a great mercy. A mildly venal pope would have been business as usual; the dysfunction in the curia could have festered for generations more. But Benedict, by being the worst possible pope, gave the reformers the kick they needed. The pope who succeeded Damasus II was St. Leo IX. He began a reform of the whole Church that included taking the clerical vow of celibacy seriously and cracking down on simony.

As for that honest but unhappy reformer Gregory VI, he left more of a legacy than he might have hoped. His young friend Hildebrand was elected pope in 1073. In honor of his beloved mentor, he took the name Gregory as well, and today we remember him as St. Gregory VII—one of the greatest reformers in the history of the Church. In fact, historians have a name for the period that followed the three papacies of Benedict IX: the Gregorian Renaissance.

CHAPTER EIGHT

St. Celestine V

(1294)

*T*he trail is getting steep, and the already weary travelers certainly aren't dressed for a hike in the woods. The long robes of the three bishops, one cardinal, two kings, and two high Roman officials catch in the thorns every few yards, and their shoes give no protection at all from the roots and rocks that stick up from the ill-kept path. The twittering birds and fluttering butterflies of the beautiful Italian countryside were charming at first; now they seem to be mocking the poorly prepared travelers. The hot July sun beats down mercilessly.

At last, hundreds of feet up from the valley, the hikers see their destination. Above the pathway, on a rock sticking out of the face of the mountain, is a little stone cell, not big enough for a man to stand up in. A hole in the front is covered by an iron grating. A crowd of people of every description already fills every flat space nearby. They're all waiting to see what will happen when the dignitaries reach the ledge.

The weary, smelly, perspiring dignitaries climb up the last few yards and peer in through the grating. There, in the cool darkness of his little cave, is an ancient man, skeletally thin, with a long and stringy white beard, wearing a sort of coarse hair tunic he obviously made himself out of the most wretched materials. His eyes gleam out of the darkness; he looks like a rabbit caught in a trap.

The kings, bishops, and notaries all take off their hats and kneel on the hard stone in front of the grating. One of them—the archbishop of Lyon—holds out a roll of parchment with an impressive seal.

"Under the guidance of the Holy Spirit," he declares to the frightened-looking wild man in the cave, "the college of cardinals, by unanimous vote, has chosen you as pope."

• • •

The election was one of the most difficult in the history of the papacy. It took two years and three months. For some of that time the cardinals jockeyed for position; for some of it they were scattered all over Italy and would not talk to one another. One historian said the cardinals of the time might better be called *carnals*, since most of them cared more for their earthly ambitions than for the Church. There is good evidence of bribery by secular rulers, which doubtless made the stalemate even harder to break.

There were only twelve cardinals at that time, and at least two-thirds of them had to vote for a candidate to make him pope. But not even four could agree.

Meanwhile the city of Rome was in chaos. By tradition, all prisoners were released during a *sede vacante*, a time when the pope's chair was vacant. The people of Rome usually ended up rioting uncontrollably during such periods. As the *sede vacante* dragged on, the riots grew worse, practically resulting in civil war. The gangs associated with the ruling families, always ready to slaughter each other on the slightest provocation, fought pitched battles in the streets. The highest government officials fled the city. Churches were plundered.

As if that weren't bad enough, the other cities in the papal territories started fighting their own little wars. Each bigger town thought it might take advantage of this golden opportunity to squash its smaller neighbor. The cardinals were constantly distracted from the business of electing a pope by the business of directing troop movements hither and yon in an increasingly futile attempt to stamp out the rebellions and wars throughout central Italy.

And then the plague came. One of the cardinals died from it, leaving only eleven men to choose the next pope. Would they ever manage it?

Cardinal Latinus Malabranca was the chairman of the college. Unlike most of the others, he had a spotless reputation: No one suspected him of desiring anything but the good of the Church. He managed to gather nine of the eleven cardinals together for a serious talk.

"I've had a letter from a very holy man," he told them. "He's been told in a vision that God will punish us, the cardinals, unless we choose a pope as soon as possible."

"Is that your friend Peter of Morrone?" asked Cardinal Gaetani with a hint of sarcasm in his voice. It was no secret that Cardinal Gaetani, a powerful nobleman, wanted the chair of Peter for himself, and he looked on the pronouncements of an ignorant hermit with undisguised contempt.

"Yes," Cardinal Latinus answered. "Peter, the holy hermit of Morrone."

"I've heard marvelous things about him," one of the other cardinals remarked. The cardinals began to trade stories they had heard about this strange hermit—his wonderfully ascetic life, the monasteries he had founded, the churches he had managed to have restored or built, and the miracles people said happened when he was near.

Suddenly Cardinal Latinus stated in a loud voice: "In the name of the Father, and of the Son, and of the Holy Spirit, I cast my vote for Peter of Morrone!"

There was shocked silence. Then another cardinal spoke up: "I cast my vote for Peter of Morrone!" Almost immediately four more voices joined the chorus.

The rest of the cardinals came around one by one. The two who were missing from the meeting were sent for, and when they heard what had happened, they also concluded that this was indeed the only way to break the stalemate, and they added their votes for the hermit Peter.

Every cardinal had a similar thought: *My* side doesn't win, but at least *their* side doesn't win either. The venal bickering and selfishness of the cardinals had led them to elect a saint.

• • •

The cardinals decided not meet Peter in person. Were they having second thoughts? Or were they just afraid to travel in the unsettled conditions the long *sede vacante* had created? Whatever the reason, they ended up sending three bishops and two Roman notaries on the arduous journey to Peter's cell.

Meanwhile, news of the unanimous election, after more than two years of deadlock, traveled fast. King Charles of Naples already knew the holy hermit of Morrone and in fact had done him a few favors when he needed help for his monastic brethren. Now he decided to be among the first to greet the new pope—partly, perhaps, because he was a pious king, but also because he suspected that Peter would be baffled by his new position and easily influenced by whoever got there first. Since the papal territories bordered on the Kingdom of Naples, controlling the mind of the pope would be equivalent to doubling Charles's territory. And so King Charles and his son Charles, who had recently become king of Hungary by marriage, made their way to meet the new pope.

One of the cardinals also ruminated on how easily the new pope might be influenced by strong personalities. Peter Colonna decided that the one thing he could not allow was that the hated Orsini family—to which two of the other cardinals belonged—should get to the new pope first. Not as a representative of the college of cardinals but strictly on his own account, Peter Colonna headed for Morrone.

News had also reached the part of the Abruzzi where the new pope had his cell, and the people of the countryside were overjoyed. The monks who had loosely surrounded the hermit were especially happy. They had been afraid their new order would be suppressed by the previous pope, and now their leader was pope. The unanimous election seemed nothing less than a miracle.

The only man in the Abruzzi who wasn't happy about the election was the hermit himself. "Who am I to carry a burden like this?" he asked when the news reached his little cave. His fellow monks told him that the Holy Spirit, and no human power, had chosen him to lead the Church, and it would be going against God to refuse. But Peter looked at himself and did not see pope material. He decided to run away.

The people of the countryside would have none of that. Their own holy man was going to be pope, whether he liked it or not. They very respectfully hauled him back to his cell and, with the utmost deference, set up a guard to make sure he didn't try to slip away again.

Meanwhile, the official delegates drew near. Hundreds, maybe thousands of people from the surrounding countryside turned out to catch a glimpse of the historic moment. When the official announcement was made, the scraggly hermit asked leave to pray. Then he consented to be led down the mountain to the monastery nearby.

• • •

The new pope was not very sure of himself; he seems to have wavered again. He decided to refuse the papacy after all, until the wise and incorruptible Cardinal Malabranca came and persuaded him that the Church would be in bad shape if he did.

The old hermit decided to rely on experts rather than on his own administrative ability in secular matters. The most commanding presence among the experts who willingly offered their advice was King Charles of Naples. This was bad news to the cardinals. They didn't agree on most things, but a solid majority of them did not trust King Charles. How they wished they had all come in person to deliver the news of the election! But it was too late now.

The new pope announced his intention to be crowned in Aquila, a nearby city in the Kingdom of Naples. He said he was too old and frail to come to the cardinals at Perugia, where they were at the moment, or to Rome itself. The cardinals shook their heads: King Charles was behind this. He knew that most of them were afraid even to set foot in his kingdom, frosty as relations had been between Naples and the papal dominions.

The new pope's entry into Aquila made for a strange sight. Against all advice, Celestine insisted on riding on a humble donkey. The upper-class ecclesiastics were appalled; the ordinary people, however, were delighted. Eyewitnesses tell us that two hundred thousand of them turned out to jostle for a view of the wonderful new pope who imitated Christ's humility. They cheered wildly as he rode by on his little donkey, with a king walking on each side to hold the reins.

The new pope's choice of the name Celestine (the fifth of that name) was symbolic. The name pointed to heaven rather than to earth.

Almost immediately Celestine set out on a course of change that horrified the ecclesiastical establishment. He refused to go to Rome but instead ended up in the palace of his friend King Charles of Naples, where he was treated with the utmost deference and laughed at behind his back. In the king's palace Celestine made himself a tiny cell, where he could live something like the life he had loved in his little cave. There were times when king and cardinals had trouble dragging him back to his throne to do pope stuff.

Celestine appointed his friends the simple monks to high positions in the Church, which did not go over well at all with the Italian nobility. The wise old Cardinal Malabranca died, and Celestine chose a French archbishop to replace him as dean of the college of cardinals—which infuriated the Italians. They saw the influence of Charles, the son of the former king of France and the brother of the current one.

Celestine more than doubled the college of cardinals—and not one of the new appointees was a Roman. More than half of them were French, in fact. Doubtless, the Roman faction thought, Charles was behind that too.

Then Celestine reenacted the conclave law of Pope Gregory X's time: When the pope died, the cardinals would have to gather where he had died—whether it was in Rome or at the palace of the King of Naples— within ten days. They would assemble *cum clave*—with a key. (That's where our word *conclave* comes from.) They would literally be locked in until they had chosen a new pope, and no one would be able to enter or leave. Their food would have to be passed through a slot too narrow for a human to go through.

The cardinals hated that rule. It left no room for exercising influence. King Charles hoped that, by keeping the pope in his palace until he died and stuffing the college with friendly cardinals, he would completely control a future election. But in fact the reform was permanent. Celestine was the last pope elected outside a conclave.

• • •

The humble saint was not having any fun as pope. He hated the politics, he hated the corruption, and most of all he hated the pomp and magnificence that went with the office. Surrounded by temptations to luxury, he feared for his immortal soul. A story circulated that he was hearing a terrifying voice in the middle of the night telling him that he must flee from temptation—a voice, the story said, that actually belonged to a young cleric bellowing through a hidden hole that Cardinal Gaetani had drilled into the pope's chamber. The story was so persistent that, more than a century later, the Middle English poet John Gower used it to represent the sin of envy in his *Confessio Amantis*, or *Lover's Confession*, a long poem about the seven deadly sins.

> This cardinal, with cunning guile,
> On one day, when he had a while,
> Unto himself this young clerk took,
> And made him swear upon a book,
> And told him what he planned to do.
> "This trumpet that I give to you—
> Wait, and the deepest silence keep,
> Until the pope is fast asleep,
> And you are sure no one is nigh,
> And then you must be very sly:
> Speak through the trumpet in his ears
> So that the pope will think he hears
> A voice from heaven speaking plain,
> And, meditating in his brain,
> Remembers it when he has woken,
> And thinks that God himself has spoken."[59]

King Charles feared that Celestine might resign and thus deprive him of the opportunity of controlling the papacy. He encouraged the people of Naples to stage a huge demonstration begging the pope to stay on. When they assembled under the windows of the palace, they were told that they had been heard—the pope would not resign.

But then, without warning, he did. He called all the cardinals together and told them he understood what a miserable pope he had been: His unsophisticated manners, thick accent, and lack of management experience made it impossible for him to be what a pope ought to be. All he had ever wanted was to serve God in his own humble way.

Celestine was so obviously miserable that the cardinals, who had been joining in the jokes behind his back, were all in tears. They persuaded him to stay on long enough to issue a declaration that the pope might lay down his office if he chose, and then they accepted his retirement.

This time it took only ten days to come up with a new pope. Cardinal Gaetani masterfully played the factions against one another, speaking to them privately, persuading them to agree to leave the nomination to him, with subtle hints that the nomination would go their way if they did. Then he nominated himself.

Gaetani rode the finest horse in Naples to his coronation. He took the name Boniface VIII, a name that means "Doing Good." It suggested that he intended to be known by his deeds.

• • •

The retired Pope Celestine thought he could go back to being a hermit, but Pope Boniface would not allow it. The most charitable interpretation is that Boniface was afraid of a schism in the Church. He saw Celestine as a simpleton who might be persuaded by unscrupulous followers that his abdication was not legitimate; then he might declare himself pope again, and there would be two popes. The only way to avoid schism was to make sure that Celestine didn't try to retrieve the papacy.

Celestine showed no inclination to take up the crown again. He escaped from his close supervision and went straight back to his little cave in the mountains. Boniface was not amused; he had the old man dragged to Rome and kept in close confinement in what amounted to a dungeon cell. The location was dreadfully unhealthy: Friends of the ex-pope had to stop visiting him because many of them became ill. Soon all question of rivalry was moot; the retired pope died—perhaps of mistreatment, perhaps of disease, or perhaps just of old age.

Or perhaps he was murdered: There is a hole in Celestine's skull that looks a bit suspicious. Did a guard think he would do the new pope a favor by getting rid of the old one?

Celestine was given a magnificent funeral, bankrolled by his successor. The magnificence was a sign to everyone that he was really dead—a message Boniface wanted to broadcast to all of Europe. The body was laid to rest in a fine tomb in the basilica at Aquila—a basilica whose construction the hermit Peter had arranged before he became pope.

As for Pope Boniface, the wily Roman insider used every trick he could think of to increase the power of the papacy, and he pretty much botched everything. Like Celestine before him, he ended up fleeing, being caught, and dying in a prison cell. The French influence in the college of cardinals would soon result in a series of popes who refused to go to Rome. They would stay at Avignon, a papal territory in the south of France. Italians were appalled, of course, but the move did get the popes away from the constant gang warfare that surrounded them in Rome. It was nearly seventy years before the popes moved back to the Eternal City.

Almost immediately after Boniface died, Celestine was canonized a saint—partly because of a groundswell of popular feeling and partly because Boniface's enemies saw it as one last way to poke him in the eye. Even after death Celestine seemed to do God's work by harnessing people's tawdriest impulses.

Celestine's legacy still provokes heated arguments among historians. No one really doubts that he was a saint—but was he a good pope? Many say that he was not: He was too simpleminded and was easily led by stronger personalities to do terribly destructive things that practically ruined the papacy. Worse than that for the poet Dante was that his resignation paved the way for Boniface VIII, and Dante hated Boniface. In his *Inferno* he sees in the first circle of hell, where spirits of those who were neither good nor bad shuffle about in eternal gloom, "the shade of him who through his cowardice made the great refusal,"[60] a line that almost all critics take as referring to Celestine V. (Dante puts Boniface VIII way down in the eighth circle of hell, where he has more than gloom to worry about.)

On the other hand, Celestine might not have been so simple. The less cynical might say that the papal court needed a sledgehammer, and Celestine brought one. He broke the power of the Roman gangs who had controlled the papacy for generations. He made sure that no papal election would ever again take place outside a conclave. These are not trivial accomplishments: Other popes, whom historians regard as far more competent, had tried to do the same things and utterly failed.

In 2009 a terrible earthquake struck Aquila. The basilica St. Celestine had built was badly damaged, but St. Celestine's remains were untouched—another miracle for the sainted pope, some said. In the following days Pope Benedict XVI visited the site to see for himself what the people of Aquila had suffered. When he reached the casket of St. Celestine, he left a gift: the pallium in which he himself had been crowned pope in 2005.

CHAPTER NINE

Alexander VI

(1492–1503)

"*N*one of those who preceded or followed him have shown like him what a pontiff can do with men and money."[61] So wrote Machiavelli, who admired Alexander as the pattern of a successful ecclesiastical tyrant. Men and money—those were the things Rodrigo Borgia understood. Theology was largely a thing he left alone.

Rodrigo Borja (the Spanish form of the name) was born in Spain in 1431. His family was a powerful one; his uncle Alfonso Borgia became Pope Callixtus III, making Rodrigo's rise in the Church meteoric. He eventually became archbishop of Valencia, and from there he was elected to the papacy in 1492, taking the name Alexander VI.

An old legend says that the sixteen-year-old Cardinal Giovanni de' Medici told his friends, "Run away! We're in the grip of a wolf!"[62] (Giovanni would later become Pope Leo X.) If a member of the powerful and hardly sheepish Medici family was afraid of him, the new pope must have been formidable.

But perhaps a formidable pope was what was needed at the time. In the 1400s Italy was a motley collection of kingdoms and republics, but the most powerful secular ruler in Italy was the pope. He commanded armies and did not hesitate to send them into battle to protect or enlarge his kingdom. It often seemed as though his secular responsibilities overshadowed his spiritual ones.

Naturally, the most powerful kingdoms of the time vied to get their own candidates in the chair of Peter. But the Borgias, who were derided by their enemies as greedy schemers and praised by their supporters as successful schemers, were more or less neutral—a good counterbalance, perhaps, to the rival powers that overshadowed Italy.

Alexander was certainly a worldly sort of bishop. He had a number of mistresses. His favorite bore him two sons, Giovanni and Cesare, and a daughter, Lucretia, whom rivals of the Borgias would accuse of multiple poisonings and other malicious deeds.

Cesare Borgia was made bishop of Pamplona in Spain at the age of fourteen. When his father became pope, Cesare was eighteen years old, not too young to be made a cardinal. It was a good career path for a second son. Alexander expected his older son, Giovanni (or Juan), to carry on the family empire. Cesare was not very interested in his clerical duties, but then neither was his father the pope.

Giovanni didn't last long. We hear the curious story from Bishop Johannes Burchardus, who became Alexander's pontifical master of ceremonies and kept a diary of affairs in the papal court and the city of Rome. The story is worth reading at length, both because it's a well-told tale and because it gives us a vivid picture of what Rome was like under the worldly popes.

> On Wednesday, the 14th of June, 1497, Cesare Borgia and Juan Borgia, Duke of Aragon, the Captain General of the guards, the favorite sons of the pope, dined at the house of Donna Vanozza, their mother, who lived in the neighborhood of the

Church of Saint Peter in Chains. Their mother and various other people were present at the dinner. After the meal, when night had fallen, Cesare urged his brother to return to the Apostolic palace. And so they both mounted the horses or mules with a few attendants, as they had not many servants with them, and rode together until they approached the neighborhood of the palace of the Vice-chancellor Ascanio Sforza, which the Pope had erected and usually occupied during his tenure of the office of Vice-chancellor.

At this point the duke declared that he would like to find entertainment somewhere and took leave of his brother, the Cardinal. He dismissed all his servants except one and retained further a masked man who had already presented himself before the dinner and had visited him in the Apostolic palace almost every day for a month. The duke took him up behind him on his mule and rode to the Square of the Jews, where he dismissed the one groom and sent him back to the palace. He instructed him, however, that he should wait for him about eight o'clock in the square, and if he had not appeared at the end of an hour he should return to the palace. Thereupon the duke departed from the groom, with the masked man behind him on the back of the mule, and rode no one knows whither and was murdered.

The corpse was thrown into the river at the point beside the fountain where the refuse of the streets is usually dumped into the water, near or beside the Hospital of Saint Hieronymus of the Slavonians on the road which runs from the Angel's Bridge straight to the Church of Santa Maria del Popolo. The groom who had been dismissed on the Square of the Jews was hurt seriously and wounded unto death. He was mercifully taken into the house of someone unknown to me and cared for. Unconscious as he was, he could tell nothing about his instructions and the expedition of his master.

When the duke did not return to the palace on the next morning, which was Thursday, the 15th of June, his trusted servants became uneasy, and one of them carried to the Pope the news of the late expedition of the duke and Cesare and the vain watch for the duke's return. The Pope was much disturbed at the news, but tried to persuade himself that the duke was enjoying himself somewhere with a girl and was embarrassed for that reason at leaving her house in broad daylight, and he clung to the hope that he might return at any rate in the evening. When this hope was not fulfilled, the Pope was stricken with deadly terror and set on foot all possible inquiries through a few of his trusted men.

Among those who were questioned was a Slavonian dealer in wood by the name of Georgio, who had unloaded his wood on the bank of the Tiber near the above-mentioned fountain and who had spent the night on his boat guarding his wood to prevent it being stolen. The question was put to him whether he had seen anything thrown into the river during the middle of the night just past, to which he made answer that at about two o'clock in the morning two men came out of a lane by the hospital on to the public road along the river. They looked about cautiously to see whether any one was passing, and when they did not see anybody, they disappeared again in the lane. After a little while two others came out of the lane, looked about in the same way and made a sign to their companions when they discovered nobody. Thereupon a rider appeared on a white horse who had a corpse behind him with the head and arms hanging down on one side and the legs on the other and supported on both sides by the two men who had first appeared. The procession advanced to the place where the refuse is thrown into the river. At the bank they came to a halt and turned the horse with its tail to the river. Then they lifted the corpse, one holding it by its hands and arms, the other by the legs and feet, dragged it down from the horse and cast it with all their strength into the river.

When the rider asked if it was safely in, they answered, "Yes, Sir!" Then the rider cast another look at the river and, seeing the cloak of the corpse floating on the water, asked his companions what that black thing was floating there. They answered, "the cloak," whereupon he threw stones at the garment to make it sink to the bottom. Then all five, including the other two who had kept watch and now rejoined the rider and his two companions, departed and took their way together through another lane that leads to the Hospital of Saint James.

The servants of the Pope asked Giorgio why he had lodged no information of such a crime with the governor of the city, to which he answered: "In my day I have seen as many as a hundred corpses thrown into the river at that place on different nights without anybody troubling himself about it, and so I attached no further importance to the circumstance."

After this fishermen and boatmen were summoned from all Rome and ordered to drag the corpse out of the river with the assurance of a large reward for their pains.

Three hundred fishermen and boatmen, as I have heard, came together and dragged the bed of the river, and finally brought up the corpse of a man. It was just before vespers when they found the duke still fully clad, with his stockings, shoes, coat, waistcoat and cloak, and in his belt there was his purse with thirty ducats. He had nine wounds, one in the neck through the throat, the other eight in the head, body and legs. The duke was laid in a boat and was carried into the castle of San Angelo, where his clothing was removed. The corpse was then washed and clothed in princely raiment. Everything was done at the order of my colleague, Bernardino Gutieri, cleric in charge of ceremonies.

On the evening of this day, at nine o'clock the corpse of the duke was brought by his noble retainers, if I remember rightly, from the castle of San Angelo to the church of Santa Maria del Popolo, preceded by 120 torchbearers and all the prelates of the palace, together with the papal servitors and pages. With loud lamentations and weeping they proceeded without any orderly formation. The corpse was borne upon a bier with pomp and ceremony in public view and looked more as if sleeping than dead. In the aforementioned church it was consigned to the vault, where it reposes up to the present day.

When the Pope was informed that the duke had been murdered and thrown into the river like refuse and there discovered, violent grief overcame him, and in his deep sorrow he locked himself in his chambers and wept bitterly. Only after long pleading, persuasion and solicitation before his door did the Cardinal Bartolommeo Marti finally succeed after several hours in being admitted with a few attendants. The Pope took no food or drink from the evening of Wednesday, the 14th of June, until the following Saturday, and he let no sleep come to his eyes from the morning of Thursday until the next Sunday. Upon varied and ceaseless appeals of his trusted friends he allowed himself to be won over and finally began to conquer his grief as well as he could. This he did also out of consideration for the risk and danger to his own person.[63]

The grieving father ordered a thorough investigation into the foul murder. Then, a week later, the investigation was suddenly terminated. Why?

No one has ever conclusively solved the mystery. But many Romans then, and many historians since then, believed that the murderer was Giovanni's brother Cesare. Certainly Cesare stood to benefit from being the oldest surviving son; not long afterward he resigned as cardinal and took up a career conquering northern Italy, a career financed by his father the pope.

At any rate, the mysterious death did not disturb the Roman public very much. After Giovanni's body was hauled out of the Tiber, one Roman humorist remarked that the pope was now truly a fisher of men. It was a cruel joke, but it was probably a fair representation of the collective shrug that came from the populace of the city. People were used to such crimes among the nobility, as our diarist had mentioned when Alexander became pope:

> After his coronation it was brought to his knowledge that, from the day of the last illness of Innocent until his coronation [a period of two and a half weeks], more than two hundred and twenty men had been assassinated in various places and at various times. It was also brought to his knowledge who the murderers were and the reasons and success they had had.[64]

Rome made Dodge City in its worst days look like a nunnery. No place was safe:

> Last Sunday, the 18th, Giulio Vitelli of Corneto, a servant of Cardinal Domenico delle Rovere, was just attending Mass in the convent church of the Dominicans sopra Minerva, when some one entered the church with about ten companions in arms carrying concealed crossbows and bearing long and short swords, lances and round shields. They rushed into the Chapel of Crucifixion toward Giulio and his brothers and wounded them, and of these wounds Giulio and two of his brothers died within a few days.[65]

This was the Rome of which the pope was the secular governor, as well as the spiritual leader. Now we see, perhaps, why the cardinals might have thought that someone utterly ruthless would be a good choice for pope. Alexander may not have cared much one way or the other about religion, but he did care about his own safety. Public order was necessary to keep him safe, so he would work on restoring it.

• • •

What other stories can we tell about Alexander VI? They say he poisoned cardinals whenever he needed money. The Borgias were great poisoners, with a special love for arsenic, which worked slowly and killed its victims in a way that was hard to distinguish from natural decline. But perhaps the stories were exaggerated, and he only poisoned two or three cardinals. Alexander was never cruel from a love of cruelty. He only did what he had to do to get what he wanted, and he only did it to people who were in the way.

For example, our diarist tells us what happened to a Spanish archbishop, Alexander's own secretary. Pope Alexander had gotten on the wrong side of Ferdinand and Isabella, the powerful rulers of Spain (and sponsors of Christopher Columbus), and it was necessary that someone else take the blame for the pope's actions.

On the evening of the 28th of October, 1497, the secretary of the Pope, Bartolommeo Florido, formerly Archbishop of Cosenza, who had recently been deprived of all his honors, dignities, rank and livings in the Castle of San Angelo, was forced to lay off all his vestments. A cowl of coarse white cloth which hung down half a span below the knee was put on over his shirt instead of his tunic. He received a pair of shoes of the roughest leather, a coat of green cloth which almost reached the ground and was also very coarse and thick, and a coarse white cap. In his hands he was given a rather large wooden crucifix. In this attire he was brought from the chamber in which he had until then been held prisoner to the burial vault of the Emperor Hadrian called San Marocco, which had been designated as his life-long prison.

There stood for him a common wooden bed with a canopy to protect his head from the moisture of the stone walls. Upon the bed lay a straw pallet and a mattress with two coarse blankets. He was given a breviary, a Bible, and the letters of Saint Peter. Furthermore he received a keg of water, three loaves of bread, a cup of oil and a lamp for lighting. There he was incarcerated for the term of his life.

The Pope, as I was told, has given the order that the warden of the castle or his deputy should visit the prisoner every day or every three days and that bread and water should be portioned out to him for his maintenance and oil for his light. May Almighty God in all his mercy and loving kindness bestow upon this most miserable man the gift of patience and grant him grace that he may save his soul.

The report was that before this the Pope had daily dispatched to the imprisoned Florido in the castle of San Angelo the suffragan bishop of Toul, John Marades, the archdeacon de Bacchis, Petrus de Solis, and a few others of his trusted servants to play dice and chess with him and to lead him through proper persuasion to the confession that he had drawn up various briefs without the order of the Pope. For the Pope thought thus to obtain forgiveness for other briefs that had been drawn upon his order and had offended the King and Queen of Spain on the plea that they had been issued without his foreknowledge. If Florido would admit this, the Pope would raise his rank and reward him with higher offices. At their repeated instigation he had confessed, and thereafter neither Marades nor the others had ever visited him again.[66]

• • •

It may come as a surprise that Alexander's papacy did have its good points. First of all, he left the sacred faith intact. Alexander simply had too little interest in theology to teach heresy. He was a practical man.

As Machiavelli pointed out, Alexander was a competent administrator, and that at a time when the administration of a large secular state was a big part of the pope's duties. If something could be done with money, Alexander did it, and he improved things considerably in Rome. The constant crime spree that was daily life slowed down quite a bit, because Alexander actually did something to enforce the laws. He also made the machinery of the Roman Church run more smoothly than it had for years.

Nevertheless, on the whole, the people of Rome hated their pope. His life of scheming and open immorality was appalling, even to citizens who were used to appalling things.

Yet what a shower of blessings came down on the Church after Alexander! The worldliness of the Renaissance popes sowed the seeds of a great reform. In fact, it would be the last great reform. The papacy would never again be the plaything of noble families. Future popes would be selected on the basis of holiness and talent.

Blessings also came through the illegitimate children of Alexander. His great-grandson Francis Borgia, born just seven years after Alexander died, became the third leader of the Jesuits. He had inherited his family's knack for organization and administration, but he combined it with a remarkable personal holiness and piety. Today we remember him as St. Francis Borgia.

Some of the Borgia family moved to South America in Spanish colonial times. A direct descendant of Pope Alexander VI, Rodrigo Borja, served as president of Ecuador from 1988 to 1992.

CHAPTER TEN

St. Pius V
(1566–1572)

*T*he scene is a street in Rome. An English visitor notices a crowd forming and wonders what the fuss is about. Probably some papist folly, he thinks. He thanks heaven that England has been rescued from popery by her great and glorious Queen Elizabeth.

As he makes his way through the people, he sees that it is indeed popery that has drawn the crowd. The pope himself is there. And in front of the pope is the most revoltingly filthy beggar he has ever seen: a man dressed in a few rags and covered with festering sores.

The Englishman assumes that the impudent beggar stopped the pope to beg a few coppers, and the pope's minions will soon put him in his place. But then he sees the aged but still vigorous pope slowly *kneel* in front of the beggar. And then the pope kisses his filthy, boil-infested feet.

From that moment the Englishman is a Roman Catholic.

• • •

There had not been a bleaker hour for the Catholic Church since the Dark Ages. In northern Europe the Protestant Reformation had alienated whole nations from the Catholic Church. England and several of the German states had defected; much of Switzerland was under the sway of Calvinism; France was wavering. In the south and east, the Islamic armies of the Ottoman Empire were pushing farther and farther into Europe, threatening to take Rome itself, as they had taken Constantinople a century earlier.

The much-reduced Roman Catholic Church seemed like a city under siege. What was worse, the Protestants seemed to have seized the moral high ground in many ways. The Calvinists, for example, had transformed Geneva into a strict theocracy. It was a cold, lifeless husk of a city, but the notorious immorality that infected the Church was gone or at least not visible.

This was the world when Michele Ghisleri was elected pope in 1566. Never had the Catholic Church more desperately needed a truly good pope who was also a truly good man. Cardinal Ghisleri had pleaded with the cardinals not to choose him, but they had done so anyway, seemingly by divine inspiration.

Ghisleri had been a Dominican friar. Even when he became a bishop and then a cardinal, he was in the habit of walking rather than riding, fasting, staying up all night to pray, and in general acting more like a humble servant than like a prince. But now that he was pope, he was surrounded by all the imperial pomp put in place by the proud Medicis and Borgias. Would it change him?

The people knew right away that this pope was different. Recent popes had begun their reigns by distributing large gifts to rich friends and useful acquaintances; Pius V gave his gifts to the poor. What kind of policy was that?

The change of tone did not stop there. Pius lived in the magnificent palaces built by his predecessors, but he lived like a man who had taken a vow of poverty. Throughout his reign he would visit the bedsides of the sick, minister to lepers, and wash the feet of the poor. These things would have made the Medicis and the Borgias hold their noses in disgust.

As secular governor of his territory, the pope brought his moral revolution into the city of Rome. The bordellos were forced to move out to the suburbs. (Even the pope couldn't get rid of them altogether.) The party was over in the city, and laws were strictly enforced for the first time in generations.

Pius was not content with reforming things in the territories directly under his control. The Protestant Reformation had succeeded as much as it did partly because of the scandalously visible corruption in the Church. Pius was determined that the corruption would end. Amid much grumbling, he set about reforming the Church all over the world.

In many places the office of bishop was a source of income for second sons of noble families. These never did the work of a bishop; they simply sucked up the money from a diocese they had never seen, the way a stockholder might take income from a company whose factory he never visited. Now the bishops would have to work for the diocesan nickel. The pope required that they actually live in their dioceses.

He also demanded that the cardinals lead upright and simple lives. Again, we can imagine that there must have been more than a little grumbling. But the grumblers were at least obliged to look like Christians. New cardinals would not be the wastrel teenage sons of the nobility but the most capable and dedicated bishops.

Perhaps more than anything else, Pius V prayed. He prayed without ceasing, as Paul commands (1 Thessalonians 5:17). He was on his knees in front of the Blessed Sacrament at least twice a day. No matter how busy he was—and he was amazingly busy—he made prayer his first priority.

The new pope combined the holiness of Celestine with the almost ruthless efficiency of Alexander VI. He was in charge, and he knew how to use the power that had been given to him. And he was going to use it for good.

. . .

It's impossible to look at the papacy of Pius V without making the story into a catalogue of accomplishments. Few popes have done as much for the Church. When we consider that Pius had only six years to do it all, he begins to seem almost superhuman.

The reformed liturgy was one of his legacies. He standardized the Order of the Mass throughout the Catholic West. The rites as he promulgated them remained the norm until 1969, and they're still in use today—though now known as the extraordinary form to distinguish them from the ordinary form introduced in 1969.

Pope Pius V left a deep and lasting mark on sacred music too. Composers had gradually been discovering polyphony, which wove beautiful patterns out of multiple voices, but conservative thinkers in the Church still thought Gregorian chant was the only legitimate liturgical music. Certainly Gregorian chant is beautiful and inspiring, and in recent years monks who keep up the ancient tradition have made some bestselling albums. But Pope Pius insisted that the newer music was good too. He was a patron of the great composer Palestrina, making polyphony legitimate in the Church. All the great liturgical music of the centuries since—the beautiful Masses by Bach, Mozart, Beethoven, Verdi, and dozens of other great composers—were possible only because Pius V took a bold stand in favor of this shocking modern music that the conservatives couldn't understand.

We could easily say that Pius V saved Christendom from complete annihilation. The Ottoman Empire had never been more of a threat.

Since the fall of Constantinople in 1453, the Turks had continued to expand their dominion, and one Christian country after another had fallen into their hands. After Cyprus fell, Pope Pius V decided that the time had come to use his influence to bring the squabbling nations of Europe together to face the common enemy. He pushed, pulled, and wangled, and the result was the Holy League, an alliance of the greatest Catholic naval powers, which in 1571 set out to confront the Turks in the Gulf of Lepanto.

In the days leading up to the battle, Pius prayed fervently and unceasingly. Like Moses in the battle against the Amalekites (see Exodus 17:11–12), he often lifted his hands in prayer. He also ordered public devotions and fasting. At the very hour of battle there was a rosary procession going on in one of the city's churches.

Witnesses said that, on the day of the battle, the pope suddenly stopped his work, flung the window open, and announced, "Enough business! Our duty now is to thank God for the victory he has given the Christian army!" News of the battle had not yet come in, so this sudden inspiration was cited as a miracle when Pius V was canonized.

The battle was one of the turning points in history: Europeans now knew that they could stand up to the seemingly unstoppable Turks. In commemoration of the great deliverance, Pius added the words "Help of Christians" to the Litany of Our Lady and instituted the Feast of the Holy Rosary on October 11, the anniversary of the victory.

Pius V marks a firm line in the history of the papacy. The worldly popes had come to an end, as had nepotism. Though not every pope after Pius V was uniformly good, each would be chosen for his ability.

We could very easily say that the papacy as we know it today is the creation of St. Pius V. It seems almost miraculous that, after the Borgias and Medicis, a saint could sweep the Vatican clean.

CHAPTER ELEVEN

Pius XII

(1939–1958)

*T*he rumble is everywhere in the city. People stay indoors, where floors vibrate and china pieces rattle as the Nazi tanks go by. German soldiers are pouring into Rome, bringing Hitler's grim obsession with crackpot racial theories.

These are not the tin-plate bullies people had grown accustomed to under Mussolini. The old Fascist regime was oppressive, and intellectuals were likely to get beaten up by thugs who had an official government license for hooliganism. But the Nazis bring a brutal efficiency that the native Fascists never attempted. And immediately they begin the task that inevitably accompanies any Nazi invasion: rounding up Jews to send to the death camps.

Slowly the tanks rumble on, and the soldiers go about their appalling business. But when they come to the gates of the main synagogue in Rome—the number-one target in the Nazi pogrom—they stop dead. Commanders summon their superiors, and their superiors consult with even superior superiors. And no one knows quite what to do.

There on the gate is the Vatican seal.[67]

The seal is a mark of defiance, almost a thumbing of the ecclesiastical nose. It marks the synagogue and its grounds as Vatican territory. The Vatican is not Italy; it's a separate state—and a neutral one. The seal carries a blunt and obvious threat: To defy that seal will be to violate Vatican neutrality and to declare war against the Catholic Church. It may be true that the Vatican has no right to claim that little piece of Rome, which never belonged to it before. But do the Nazi commanders dare step across that line?

• • •

Eugenio Pacelli was the Vatican's Secretary of State when the Nazis came to power. The Nazis were already familiar with him, and they hated his guts. He had been the *nuncio* (ambassador) to Germany in the 1920s, when the Nazis were struggling toward power, and he had made dozens of public speeches condemning them. He had continued speaking out against "the superstition of a race and blood cult."[68] He was not winning friends in Hitler's inner circle.

Still, it was the current pope who was enemy number one, as far as the Nazis were concerned. Pope Pius XI never tired of pointing out what he considered the dangerous errors of the Nazi policy. Since half of Germany was Catholic, he was a confounded nuisance. And an encyclical to the German bishops had converted him from nuisance to mortal enemy in the Nazis' eyes.

The encyclical was called *Mit brennender Sorge*—"With Burning Anxiety." (The title of an encyclical is taken from its first two or three words.) Cardinal Pacelli was part of the team who wrote up the draft. The pope was going to give it the title *Mit grosse Sorge*—"With Great Anxiety," but Cardinal Pacelli felt that the title had to be more striking, more forceful. It had to show that this was not just a statement but a call to action. He suggested changing *great* to *burning*, and that was how the encyclical went out.

The encyclical begins with an introduction (written by Cardinal Pacelli, according to most accounts) in which the pope confronted the Nazi government. Note that the official Vatican translation renders *Mit brennender Sorge* as "It is with deep anxiety," which seems weaker than the original.

> It is with deep anxiety and growing surprise that We have long been following the painful trials of the Church and the increasing vexations which afflict those who have remained loyal in heart and action in the midst of a people [the Germans] that once received from St. Boniface the bright message and the Gospel of Christ and God's Kingdom. [69]

The encyclical goes on to attack the core of the problem: the Nazi race mythology that made Germans the so-called master race and other races inferior and thus in need of subjugation. There is no place in Christian doctrine for this mythology of race, the encyclical says. The truth is the same for all races and nations.

The peak of the revelation as reached in the Gospel of Christ is final and permanent. It knows no retouches by human hand; it admits no substitutes or arbitrary alternatives such as certain leaders pretend to draw from the so-called myth of race and blood. [70]

One of the Nazis' pet projects was the creation of a new Christianity amputated from its Jewish roots, a Christianity that rejected the Old Testament and made way for Nazi race mythology. The encyclical calls that by its name: blasphemy.

> Whoever wishes to see banished from church and school the Biblical history and the wise doctrines of the Old Testament,

blasphemes the name of God, blasphemes the Almighty's plan of salvation, and makes limited and narrow human thought the judge of God's designs over the history of the world: he denies his faith in the true Christ, such as He appeared in the flesh, the Christ who took His human nature from a people that was to crucify Him; and he understands nothing of that universal tragedy of the Son of God who to His torturer's sacrilege opposed the divine and priestly sacrifice of His redeeming death, and made the new alliance the goal of the old alliance, its realization and its crown.[71]

The language becomes even more vigorous as the encyclical attacks the Nazi propaganda machine directly:

Thousands of voices ring into your ears a Gospel which has not been revealed by the Father of Heaven. Thousands of pens are wielded in the service of a Christianity, which is not of Christ. Press and wireless daily force on you productions hostile to the Faith and to the Church, impudently aggressive against whatever you should hold venerable and sacred. Many of you, clinging to your Faith and to your Church, as a result of your affiliation with religious associations guaranteed by the concordat [the brittle agreement the Vatican had reached with Germany], have often to face the tragic trial of seeing your loyalty to your country misunderstood, suspected, or even denied, and of being hurt in your professional and social life. We are well aware that there is many a humble soldier of Christ in your ranks, who with torn feelings, but a determined heart, accepts his fate, finding his one consolation in the thought of suffering insults for the name of Jesus (Acts

5:41). Today, as We see you threatened with new dangers and new molestations, We say to you: If any one should preach to you a Gospel other than the one you received on the knees of a pious mother, from the lips of a believing father, or through teaching faithful to God and His Church, "let him be anathema" (Galatians 1:9).[72]

Nevertheless, there is a clear indication that the language is not as strong as the pope and bishops might have liked to use. The whole story of Vatican relations with the Nazis is told in two sentences:

> We have weighed every word of this letter in the balance of truth and love. We wished neither to be an accomplice to equivocation by an untimely silence, nor by excessive severity to harden the hearts of those who live under Our pastoral responsibility; for Our pastoral love pursues them none the less for all their infidelity.[73]

Could the Church win more by condemning the Nazis beyond all possibility of reconciliation or by leaving the way of reconciliation open to all erring children? There is really only one Christian answer to the question. The encyclical made clear exactly what was wrong with what the Nazis were doing, but it left open the possibility that the German government could mellow and reform. We know that didn't happen, but there was no way for Pope Pius, Cardinal Pacelli, and others in the Church to know the course of future events.

• • •

Of course, Hitler would never allow anything like this encyclical to be published in Germany. The distribution had to be done in secret. The encyclical was brought quietly into the country, and Catholic presses printed it in secret. No one knew what was happening until copies suddenly appeared throughout Germany.

Hitler was furious. The Gestapo showed up at every diocesan office in Germany and seized all copies of the encyclical that could be found. Every publisher that had printed the encyclical was seized and shut down. The government even restricted the amount of paper the Church could use.

Then began a propaganda campaign ordered by Hitler himself. The newspapers were not allowed to mention the encyclical at all; rather front pages were full of trials of monks on charges of homosexuality and pedophilia. Movies about evil priests were financed by the government and shown to children at Hitler Youth meetings—and every boy was required to be part of the Hitler Youth (including young Joseph Ratzinger, later Pope Benedict XVI, who remembers very clearly the barrage of anti-Catholic propaganda he was subjected to). Hitler thought he could destroy the reputation of the Church by painting its most visible representatives as incorrigible perverts.

When Pope Pius XI died early in 1939, rumors circulated that Eugenio Pacelli was the front-runner to replace him. The Nazis and the Fascists protested vigorously that it would be a very bad idea for the cardinals to elect someone who was so obviously prejudiced against the enlightened modern governments of Germany and Italy. But the cardinals were deaf to the protests. Eugenio Pacelli did become pope. And taking the name Pius XII sent a strong message that he intended to carry on in his predecessor's footsteps.

• • •

The new pope's first encyclical, *Summi Pontificatus*, was a direct attack on Nazi race mythology—even more direct than the attack in *Mit brennender Sorge*. The pope stated the unity of the human race so unequivocally that current theologians often turn first to *Summi Pontificatus* when they want to explain the Catholic position on race.

Among the many errors which derive from the poisoned source of religious and moral agnosticism, We would draw your attention, Venerable Brethren, to two in particular, as being those which more than others render almost impossible, or at least precarious and uncertain, the peaceful intercourse of peoples.

The first of these pernicious errors, widespread today, is the forgetfulness of that law of human solidarity and charity which is dictated and imposed by our common origin and by the equality of rational nature in all men, to whatever people they belong, and by the redeeming Sacrifice offered by Jesus Christ on the Altar of the Cross to His Heavenly Father on behalf of sinful mankind.

In fact, the first page of the Scripture, with magnificent simplicity, tells us how God, as a culmination to His creative work, made man to His Own image and likeness (see Genesis 1:26, 27); and the same Scripture tells us that He enriched man with supernatural gifts and privileges, and destined him to an eternal and ineffable happiness. It shows us besides how other men took their origin from the first couple, and then goes on, in unsurpassed vividness of language, to recount their division into different groups and their dispersion to various parts of the world. Even when they abandoned their Creator, God did not cease to regard them as His children, who, according to His merciful plan, should one day be reunited once more in His friendship (see Genesis 12:3).

The Apostle of the Gentiles later on makes himself the

herald of this truth which associates men as brothers in one great family, when he proclaims to the Greek world that God "hath made of one, all mankind, to dwell upon the whole face of the earth, determining appointed times, and the limits of their habitation, that they should seek God" (Acts 17:26, 27).

A marvelous vision, which makes us see the human race in the unity of one common origin in God "one God and Father of all, Who is above all, and through all, and in us all" (Ephesians 4:6); in the unity of nature which in every man is equally composed of material body and spiritual, immortal soul; in the unity of the immediate end and mission in the world; in the unity of dwelling place, the earth, of whose resources all men can by natural right avail themselves, to sustain and develop life; in the unity of the supernatural end, God Himself, to Whom all should tend; in the unity of means to secure that end....

In the light of this unity of all mankind, which exists in law and in fact, individuals do not feel themselves isolated units, like grains of sand, but united by the very force of their nature and by their internal destiny, into an organic, harmonious mutual relationship which varies with the changing of times.

And the nations, despite a difference of development due to diverse conditions of life and of culture, are not destined to break the unity of the human race, but rather to enrich and embellish it by the sharing of their own peculiar gifts and by that reciprocal interchange of goods which can be possible and efficacious only when a mutual love and a lively sense of charity unite all the sons of the same Father and all those redeemed by the same Divine Blood....

Our immediate predecessor, of holy and venerated memory, applying such norms to a particularly delicate question, took some generous decisions which are a monument to his insight and to the intensity of his apostolic spirit. Nor need We tell you, Venerable Brethren, that We intend to proceed without hesitation along this way. Those who enter the Church, whatever be their origin or their speech, must know that they have equal rights as children in the House of the Lord, where the law of Christ and the peace of Christ prevail.

In accordance with these principles of equality, the Church devotes her care to forming cultured native clergy and gradually increasing the number of native Bishops. And in order to give external expression to these, Our intentions, We have chosen the forthcoming Feast of Christ the King to raise to the Episcopal dignity at the Tomb of the Apostles twelve representatives of widely different peoples and races. In the midst of the disruptive contrasts which divide the human family, may this solemn act proclaim to all Our sons, scattered over the world, that the spirit, the teaching and the work of the Church can never be other than that which the Apostle of the Gentiles preached: "putting on the new, (man) him who is renewed unto knowledge, according to the image of him that created him. Where there is neither Gentile nor Jew, circumcision nor uncircumcision, barbarian nor Scythian, bond nor free. But Christ is all and in all" (Colossians 3:10, 11).[74]

It would be hard to imagine how, within the limits of Christian charity, the Holy Father could more strongly rebuke Nazi race policies.

Even so, since he was new on the job, the Nazis thought they might have an opportunity to steer Pope Pius XII away from the confrontational attitude of Pius XI. Joachim von Ribbentrop, the Nazi foreign minister, was given an audience with Pope Pius XII in 1940, and he used that time to dwell on the inevitability of the Nazi victory. Wouldn't the Church like to be on the winning side?

In reply the pope opened up a big record book on his desk and began to read from it. It was filled with the names of Polish priests, monks, and nuns murdered by the Nazis under their occupation. That was all the pope had to say. Von Ribbentrop left fuming to report that there was no reasoning with this new pope.

• • •

As the war grew bigger, the pope had to make more and more painful decisions. Lives would be lost no matter what he did. One incident, perhaps more than any other, taught him what it meant to deal with the Nazis.

In 1942 the bishops in occupied Holland made a public protest against the deportation of Dutch Jews. The Nazis responded by rounding up and murdering almost a hundred prominent converts to the Catholic Church, including St. Edith Stein, a respected philosopher who had converted from Judaism to Christianity and become a Carmelite nun (Sr. Teresa Benedicta of the Cross). It was a clear and cynical message: If you protest against our killing the Jews, then we will kill the Jews and you as well.

The killings gave the pope nightmares; his friends had seldom seen him so shaken. Clearly, in the short run at least, every public protest would kill Catholics and not save a single Jew. How could he respond?

The pope decided to be sneaky. Orders went out to convents and churches to hide as many of their Jewish neighbors as possible.

Wherever the Nazi shadow fell across Europe, monks and nuns sprang into action.

Did they do enough? No; it was impossible to do enough. They saved a few hundred thousand, but they were unarmed contemplatives pitched against the most brutally efficient killing machine ever constructed by fiendish ingenuity.

The war dragged on, and it started to go worse for the Axis powers—especially Italy. In 1943 the Fascist government collapsed. Almost immediately the Nazis invaded northern Italy and occupied Rome. Then the roundup began.

The Vatican was still technically neutral. Convents and churches all over Rome were claimed (on no legal grounds) as "extraterritorial" holdings of the Vatican, taking them outside Italian jurisdiction and thus outside the reach of the Nazi occupation. Handwritten notes from the pope went to all the monasteries and convents, telling them to open their doors to Jewish refugees. Nuns slept in basements so refugees could have their beds. Nearly five hundred Jews found shelter inside the Vatican (where the staff somehow managed to provide kosher food for them). The pope's country retreat, Castel Gandolfo, harbored about three thousand Jews. More than four thousand were hidden in other Church properties around Rome.

Herbert Kappler, the SS officer in charge of rounding up all the enemies of the Nazis, was furious when he found out about the underground network that Monsignor Hugh O'Flaherty, a high official in the Vatican, was coordinating. Kappler had a white line drawn to mark the border of Vatican City, and he announced that Msgr. O'Flaherty would be shot on sight if he stepped across it. He tried to have his agents assassinate O'Flaherty, but the Irish priest was too slippery for them.

About a thousand of Rome's Jews were rounded up and sent to death camps. But five thousand survived by hiding in Church properties that the Nazis didn't dare violate. And that's not counting those who were sheltered outside Rome, in Castel Gandolfo. Nearly four thousand others were hidden away in Christian homes.

When at last Rome was liberated by American forces, General Mark Clark apologized for the noise of his tanks. "Any time you come to liberate Rome," the pope answered with a smile, "you can make just as much noise as you like."[75]

• • •

Tributes and thanks were showered on the pope after the war. The most prominent Jewish newspapers ran editorials praising the Vatican's work in sheltering refugees from the roundup. But probably the most sincere tribute came from Israel Zolli, who had been Rome's chief rabbi during the Nazi horror. He became a Christian and entered the Catholic Church. As his baptismal name he chose Eugenio, in honor of the hero of the great rescue of Rome.

There is one more remarkable conversion worth mentioning. Herbert Kappler was arrested after the war and spent most of the rest of his life in prison. His only visitor there was Msgr. O'Flaherty, who came regularly for long and meaningful conversations. In 1959 Kappler entered the Catholic Church, baptized by the priest he had tried his best to murder fifteen years before.

CHAPTER TWELVE

John Paul II
(1978–2005)

*I*n October 1978 the weary cardinals met in conclave for the second time in two months. They had elected a relatively young pope in August, and they probably thought their work was done for ten years or more. But John Paul I died suddenly after only a month on the throne, and the cardinals were in Rome again.

Two Italians were widely considered the front-runners, but neither one of them received enough votes for the necessary majority. Then one of the cardinals suggested a compromise candidate: Karol Wojtyla, a cardinal from Poland.

It was a wildly unlikely suggestion. There had not been a pope from outside Italy since 1523. But times were changing. Pius XII had eliminated the Italian majority in the college of cardinals, and Cardinal Wojtyla was well-known to all of them as one of the great theologians of the day.

In the end he was chosen by an overwhelming majority. He was only fifty-four years old, the youngest pope of the twentieth century.

• • •

Karol Wojtyla was born in Poland in 1920. When he was only eight years old, his mother died. By the time he was twenty, he would have lost his older brother and his father as well.

In 1938 Karol went to the university in Krakow, where he showed a genius for languages. He was also very active in theater, both acting in and writing plays.

The world young Karol grew up in ended in 1939, when the Nazis and Soviets invaded and crushed Poland. The Germans immediately closed the universities; there were to be no Polish intellectuals. Slavs would be useful only as laborers. Karol worked in various menial jobs— in a chemical factory, in a quarry, in a restaurant.

But he had a new ambition. After his father's death he began to think of becoming a priest. The idea took firmer hold on him, and in 1942 he took action. He walked up to the palace of the archbishop and knocked on the door.

The only problem was that there was no seminary. All over the occupied country, Poles were meeting in secret to gain the education the Nazis tried to deny them. There was a group of young men studying for the priesthood in Krakow. Karol could join them if he could keep a secret.

The Nazi years made a profound impression on Karol. He would never forget hiding his Jewish neighbors from the roundups, hiding himself in a basement when the Nazis came looking for him, and seeing thousands of his young friends rounded up at random to prevent an uprising against the Nazis.

Liberation came, and with it opportunity for more concentrated study. In 1946 Karol Wojtyla was ordained a priest.

But it soon became clear that one occupation had succeeded another. The Soviet Union set up what was basically a puppet government in the ruins of Warsaw, and Communism was forced on Poland. The wartime alliance between the Soviets and the West quickly decayed into an armed standoff. An iron curtain, as Winston Churchill famously called it, fell across Europe.

The Communists were not as brutal as the Nazis. Officially atheist, they were not strong enough to eliminate the Catholic Church from Polish culture. Instead they made ecclesiastical life difficult.

• • •

Karol Wojtyla quickly showed himself to be one of the most capable priests in Poland. It probably came as a surprise to no one except him (he was on vacation at the time) when, at the very young age of thirty-eight, he was named a bishop. A few years later, in 1964, he was made archbishop of Krakow. Three years later he was a cardinal.

And in 1978 the cardinal from Communist Poland was elected pope.

The world was astonished. The new pope was young, he was not Italian, and he was from behind the Iron Curtain! Everything about him was unexpected. And he quickly demonstrated, in his very humble way, that things were going to change at the Vatican.

The first indication was his appearance on the balcony after his election. Such an appearance was traditional, but it was not traditional for the new pope to speak directly to the crowd. He did, in Polish-accented Italian. The crowd loved him—the first of countless crowds he would charm.

The new pope took the name John Paul II, in honor of his late friend. He wanted a simpler inauguration than the norm. There may have been grumbles from some traditionalists, but the publicity was overwhelmingly positive. Indeed, it rapidly became clear that this new pope had a real genius for publicity.

Less than a year after his election, Pope John Paul II was back in Poland for what may have been the most important papal visit in history. The Communists had run Poland into a rut, but they kept a firm grip on power. They had been appalled when a Polish pope was elected. One word from him, and the mass of Polish Catholics might rise up and throw out the Communists. At the very least there would be blood in the streets. Then the Soviet tanks would arrive, and there would be executions, which would doubtless include top figures in the Polish government.

The Communists tried to manage the pope's visit. They made detailed plans and demanded that he abide by them. Everything went smoothly, and there was no uprising.

The pope had a simple message for Poland: "Don't be afraid." The people cheered and shouted, and the Communists knew that something was happening—something that could be very bad for them. But what? The pope had done nothing they could blame him for. He had just been inspiring.

Within a year the trouble started. Workers went on strike, and soon they had formed a labor union called Solidarity. The Communists were not amused. *They* were the representatives of the workers, and no ignorant rabble was going to tell them otherwise!

Throughout the 1980s the Polish government wavered between bare tolerance of the dissident organization and a crackdown. If the Communists were to react too harshly, they risked open rebellion and Soviet tanks. If they didn't crack down hard enough, they risked open rebellion and Soviet tanks. It was not a happy time for the Communist government.

At last, in 1989, the government fell. For the first time since the Communist takeover of Eastern Europe, an Iron Curtain country had a non-Communist government. And no Soviet tanks arrived.

Following the example of Poland, one Communist government after another fell with amazing speed. By 1992 Communism was wiped off the map of Europe. How did it happen?

"The collapse of the Iron Curtain would have been impossible without John Paul II," said Mikhail Gorbachev, the last Communist leader of the Soviet Union.[76]

East and West agreed: The main force behind the collapse of Communism in Europe was the cheerful pope who told us all, "Don't be afraid."

Humble as ever, Pope John Paul II had no idea of his own power. He never expected to see the Communist world crumble in his lifetime. He simply knew that, if one had faith in God, Communists were nothing to fear.

• • •

It was not only in Europe that John Paul was a hero. Pope Paul VI had been the most traveled pope, but John Paul II made him look like a homebody. He visited countries where no pope had ever set foot before: Mexico, the Philippines, Kazakhstan, the United Kingdom. Altogether he visited 129 different countries, and everywhere he went thousands, hundreds of thousands, millions turned out to see him. In Manila for World Youth Day in 1995, he gathered a crowd of four million or more—some estimates run up to seven million. It was the largest Christian gathering in history.

This pope was a media celebrity. He could write the most profound theology, but he also knew how to work a crowd. He stood unwaveringly firm on many controversial points of Catholic theology, yet he made millions of friends among Protestants, Jews, Muslims, and people of other religions. When he took a stand, he understood how serious the issue was. And everywhere he went, he made people smile. This was the pope who inspired millions.

But nothing in the reign of John Paul II was more inspiring than his long and very public illness. It was the sort of illness we usually call debilitating, but it was not debilitating in any important way. The man was still himself, and as he became less physically capable, he showed us all that a human being is still the same human being, even if he slumps in his chair and his speech is slurred.

The world watched in a kind of awe. Many said that the pope should abdicate—he should retire and live the rest of his days in a hospital bed, perhaps, with nurses to tell him when he should turn over. There were even people—quite a number of them—who saw the pope's condition as an argument for euthanasia. Shouldn't we allow this poor man in pain to die with dignity—meaning, in a hospital bed with a needle in his arm?

Most of these people were quite sincere though sadly misguided. The pope's suffering was an inspiration to hundreds of millions of ordinary people, Catholic or not. He showed that life is worth living, even when its circumstances are difficult. And this man who would normally be considered completely disabled was still capable of leading the largest religious organization on the planet.

Pope John Paul II was always conscious of the fact that everything he did was watched, talked about, analyzed, and pondered. Like the skillful actor he was, he knew that words convey only a part of the message. Much of his public life was a silent movie, in which broad gestures told the story to people who would never hear the words. And this last act told us of the end of an earthly life in a way that moved and inspired people.

Pope John Paul II touched our hearts. He showed us joy in the face of bodily decline, a joy based on the knowledge that the decline was only a short wait on the way to infinite happiness.

Will he go down in history as John Paul the Great? It's too early to tell. History has a long reach, and none of us will live long enough to know whether the title will stick. But I sure wouldn't bet against it.

Notes

1. See NewAdvent.org for a numbered list of all the popes and the years of their reigns. "The List of Popes," *New Advent*, http://www.newadvent.org/cathen/12272b.htm.
2. Louise Ropes Loomis, trans., *The Book of the Popes (Liber Pontificales) I–* (New York: Columbia University Press, 1916), p. 5.
3. Loomis, *Book of the Popes*, p. 5.
4. C.F. Crusé, trans., *The Ecclesiastical History of Eusebius Pamphilus* (London: Bell & Daldy, 1865), pp. 173–74.
5. Eusebius, *Church History*, p. 174.
6. Eusebius, *Church History*, p. 90. St. Hegesippus was a Christian writer of the second century who cited Tradition in opposing the heresies of the Gnostics and of Marcion.
7. Eusebius, *Church History*, p. 7.
8. All quotations from the First Epistle of Clement to the Corinthians are adapted from Alexander Roberts and James Donaldson, eds., *Ante-Nicene Christian Library*, vol. 1 (Edinburgh: T. and T. Clark, 1867), p. 7.
9. Roberts and Donaldson, *Ante-Nicene Christian Library*, pp. 12, 16.
10. Roberts and Donaldson, *Ante-Nicene Christian Library*, p. 34.
11. Roberts and Donaldson, *Ante-Nicene Christian Library*, pp. 36–37.
12. Roberts and Donaldson, *Ante-Nicene Christian Library*, p. 38.
13. Roberts and Donaldson, *Ante-Nicene Christian Library*, pp. 38–39, 41–42.
14. Roberts and Donaldson, *Ante-Nicene Christian Library*, p. 47.
15. Athanasius, "Arian History," in *St. Athanasius Select Works and Letters*, eds. Philip Schaff and Henry Wace (New York: Christian Literature, 1892), p. 282.
16. Athanasius, "Arian History," p. 282.
17. Athanasius, "Arian History," p. 282.
18. Athanasius, "Arian History," p. 283.
19. Athanasius, "Arian History," p. 283.
20. Athanasius, "Arian History," pp. 283–285.
21. Athanasius, "Arian History," p. 283.
22. Theodoret, *Ecclesiastical History, Dialogues and Letters*, (New York: Christian Literature, 1892), pp. 77–79.
23. Theodoret, *Ecclesiastical History*, p. 79.
24. D.D. Yonge, trans., *The Roman History of Ammianus Marcellinus: During the Reigns of the Emperors Constantius, Julian, Jovianus, Valentinian, and Valens* (London: George Bell & Sons, 1894), p. 67.
25. Athanasius, "Arian History," p. 284.
26. Athanasius, "Arian History," pp. 284, 287.

27. Adapted from Edward Walford, trans., *The Ecclesiastical History of Sozomen: Comprising a History of the Church from AD 324 to AD 440* (London: Henry G. Bohn, 1855), p. 275.

28. Adapted from Yonge, *The Roman History of Ammianus Marcellinus*, p. 441.

29. Adapted from Yonge, *The Roman History of Ammianus Marcellinus*, p. 441.

30. Jerome, *Lives of Illustrious Men*, (New York: Christian Literature, 1892), p. 381.

31. Theodoret, *Ecclesiastical History*, p. 132.

32. Theodoret, *Ecclesiastical History*, p. 133.

33. Jerome, Letter 16. All quotations from Jerome's letters are adapted from vol. 6, *NPNF2* (New York: Christian Literature, 1893).

34. Jerome, Letter 17, p. 21.

35. Theodoret, "Letter from Damasus to the Eastern bishops," *Ecclesiastical History*, p. 139.

36. Theodoret, *Ecclesiastical History*, pp. 139–140.

37. Theodoret, *Ecclesiastical History*, p. 141.

38. Rufinus's Epilogue to Pamphilus the Martyr's Apology for Origen, in vol. 3, *NPNF2* (New York: Christian Literature, 1892), p. 426.

39. Jerome, Apology Against Rufinus, in vol. 3, *NPNF2*, p. 513.

40. Gregory Nazianzen, Letter 102, in vol. 7, *NPNF2* (New York: Christian Literature, 1894), p. 443–444.

41. Henry Hart Milman, *History of Latin Christianity* (New York: A.C. Armstrong and Son, 1889), pp. 117–118.

42. Leo I, Letter 28 "The Tome," vol. 12, *NPNF2* (New York: Christian Literature, 1895), pp. 38–40. Emphasis added.

43. Leo I, p. 43.

44. Charles Christopher Mierow, *The Gothic History of Jordanes: In English Version* (Princeton, N.J.: Princeton University Press, 1915), p. 113.

45. Mierow, *The Gothic History of Jordanes*, p. 113.

46. Mierow, *The Gothic History of Jordanes*, p. 113.

47. Mierow, *The Gothic History of Jordanes*, pp. 113–114.

48. Loomis, *Book of the Popes*, p. 152.

49. Loomis, *Book of the Popes*, p. 155.

50. Loomis, *Book of the Popes*, pp. 155–156.

51. Loomis, *Book of the Popes*, p. 156.

52. Loomis, *Book of the Popes*, p. 156.

53. Quoted in Thomas Hodgkin, *Italy and Her Invaders: The Imperial Restoration, 535–553*, (Oxford: Clarendon, 1885), pp. 662–663.

54. Author's translation of Victor III, *Cuius quidem post adeptum sacerdotium vita quam turpis, quam foeda, quamque execranda extiterit, horresco referre*, from *Dialogi de miraculis Sancti Benedicti*, p. 1141.

55. "Pope Benedict IX," *New Advent*, http://www.newadvent.org/cathen/02429a.htm.

56. Horace Kinder Mann and Johannes Hollnsteiner, *Lives of the Popes in the Early Middle Ages*, (St. Louis: K. Paul, Trench, Trübner, 1910), p. 261.

57. Quoted in Mann and Hollnsteiner, *Lives of the Popes*, p. 289.

58. See Mann and Hollnsteiner, *Lives of the Popes*, pp. 291–292.

59. John Gower, *Confessio Amantis*, in G. C. Macaulay, ed., *The Complete Works of John Gower: English Works* (Oxford: Clarendon, 1901), pp. 207–208.

60. Dante, *Inferno* Canto 3, verses 59–60. A new translation.

61. Adapted from Nicolo Machiavelli, *The Prince*, J. Scott Byerley, trans. (London: Sherwood, Neely, and Jones, 1810), p. 67.

62. Alexander Gordon, *The Lives of Pope Alexander VI and His Son Caesar Borgia* (Philadelphia: James M. Campbell, 1844), p. 25.

63. F.L. Glaser, ed., *Pope Alexander VI and His Court: Extracts from the Latin Diary of Johannes Burchardus* (New York: Nicholas L. Brown, 1921), pp. 88–93.

64. Glaser, *Pope Alexander VI and His Court*, p. 53.

65. Glaser, *Pope Alexander VI and His Court*, pp. 97–98.

66. Glaser, *Pope Alexander VI and His Court*, pp. 95–97.

67. See Thomas J. Craughwell, "Pius XII and the Holocaust," CatholicCulture.org, http://www.catholicculture.org/culture/library/view.cfm?id=316&repos=1&subrepos=0&searchid=405375.

68. Cardinal Eugenio Pacelli, quoted in Thomas J. Craughwell, *Great Rescues of World War II: Stories of Adventure, Daring, and Sacrifice* (London: Pier 9, 2009), p. 106.

69. Pius XI, *Mit brennender Sorge*, March 14, 1937, *Vatican*, para. 1, http://www.vatican.va/holy_father/pius_xi/encyclicals/documents/hf_p-xi_enc_14031937_mit-brennender-sorge_en.html.

70. Pius XI, *Mit brennender Sorge*, para. 17.

71. Pius XI, *Mit brennender Sorge*, para. 16.

72. Pius XI, *Mit brennender Sorge*, para. 33.

73. Pius XI, *Mit brennender Sorge*, para. 41.

74. Pope Pius XII, *Summi Pontificatus*, October 20, 1939, para. 34–38, 42–43, 47–48, *Vatican*, http://www.vatican.va/holy_father/pius_xii/encyclicals/documents/hf_p-xii_enc_20101939_summi-pontificatus_en.html.

75. Ronald J. Rychlak, *Hitler, the War, and the Pope* (Huntington, Ind.: Our Sunday Visitor, 2010), p. 245.

76. Alister E. McGrath, Christian History: An Introduction (Malden, Mass.: Wiley, 2013), p. 326.